# HEROIC ANIMALS
# SCARLETT BRAVES THE FLAMES
## HEROIC CAT TO THE RESCUE

BY **MATTHEW K. MANNING**          ILLUSTRATED BY **ALESSANDRO D'URSO**

CAPSTONE PRESS
a capstone imprint

Published by Capstone Press, an imprint of Capstone.
1710 Roe Crest Drive, North Mankato, Minnesota 56003
capstonepub.com

Library of Congress Cataloging-in-Publication Data
is available on the Library of Congress website.
ISBN: 9781669057710 (hardcover)
ISBN: 9781669057758 (paperback)
ISBN: 9781669057765 (ebook PDF)

Summary:
In 1996, when a fire destroyed an abandoned building in New York City, one young cat
showed incredible bravery. Scarlett was a young mother and had recently given birth to her
litter of kittens. When fire threatened her babies, she did what any mother would do—she
risked her own life to save them. Discover Scarlett's story as she braves the flames to rescue
her little ones and how they were helped by the kindness of others who found them.

Editorial Credits
Editor: Aaron Sautter; Designer: Elyse White; Media Researcher: Rebekah Hubstenberger;
Production Specialist: Whitney Schaefer

Image Credit
Associated Press: Chris Kasson, 29

All internet sites appearing in back matter were available and accurate when this book was
sent to press.

Direct quotes appear in **bold, *italicized*** text on the following pages:
Pages 15, 21: from "Extraordinary Cats," Nature, season 17, episode 8, PBS, February 21,
1999. https://www.youtube.com/watch?v=C67TUV8p2iQ

Page 27: from "Scarlett the Cat," Inside Edition, February 20, 2011. https://www.youtube.
com/watch?v=Oz9xdz1dDuk&t=9s

Printed and bound in China.  PO 5593

# TABLE OF CONTENTS

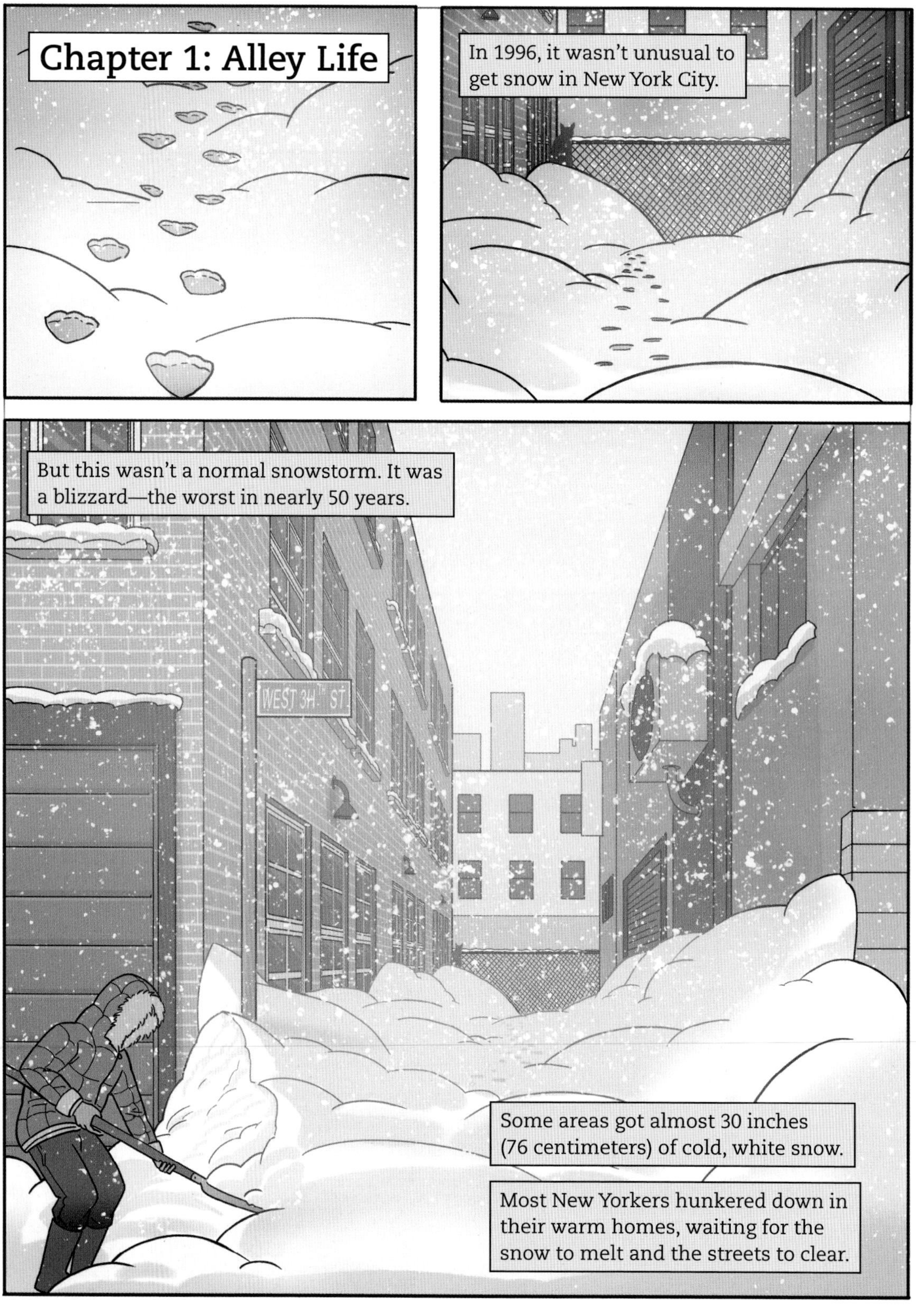
Chapter 1: Alley Life
In 1996, it wasn't unusual to get snow in New York City.
But this wasn't a normal snowstorm. It was a blizzard—the worst in nearly 50 years.
Some areas got almost 30 inches (76 centimeters) of cold, white snow.
Most New Yorkers hunkered down in their warm homes, waiting for the snow to melt and the streets to clear.

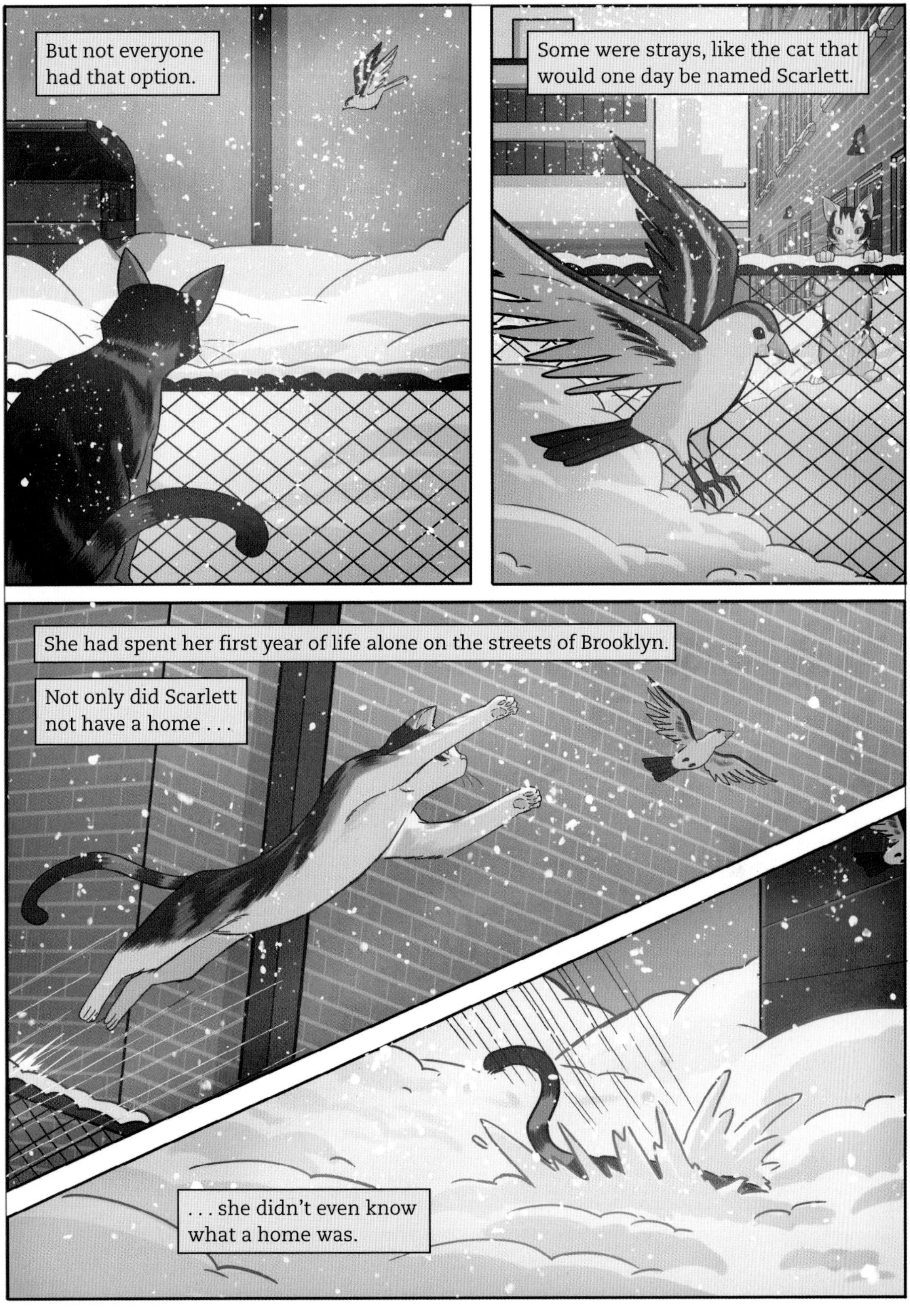
But not everyone had that option.
Some were strays, like the cat that would one day be named Scarlett.
She had spent her first year of life alone on the streets of Brooklyn.
Not only did Scarlett not have a home . . .
. . . she didn't even know what a home was.

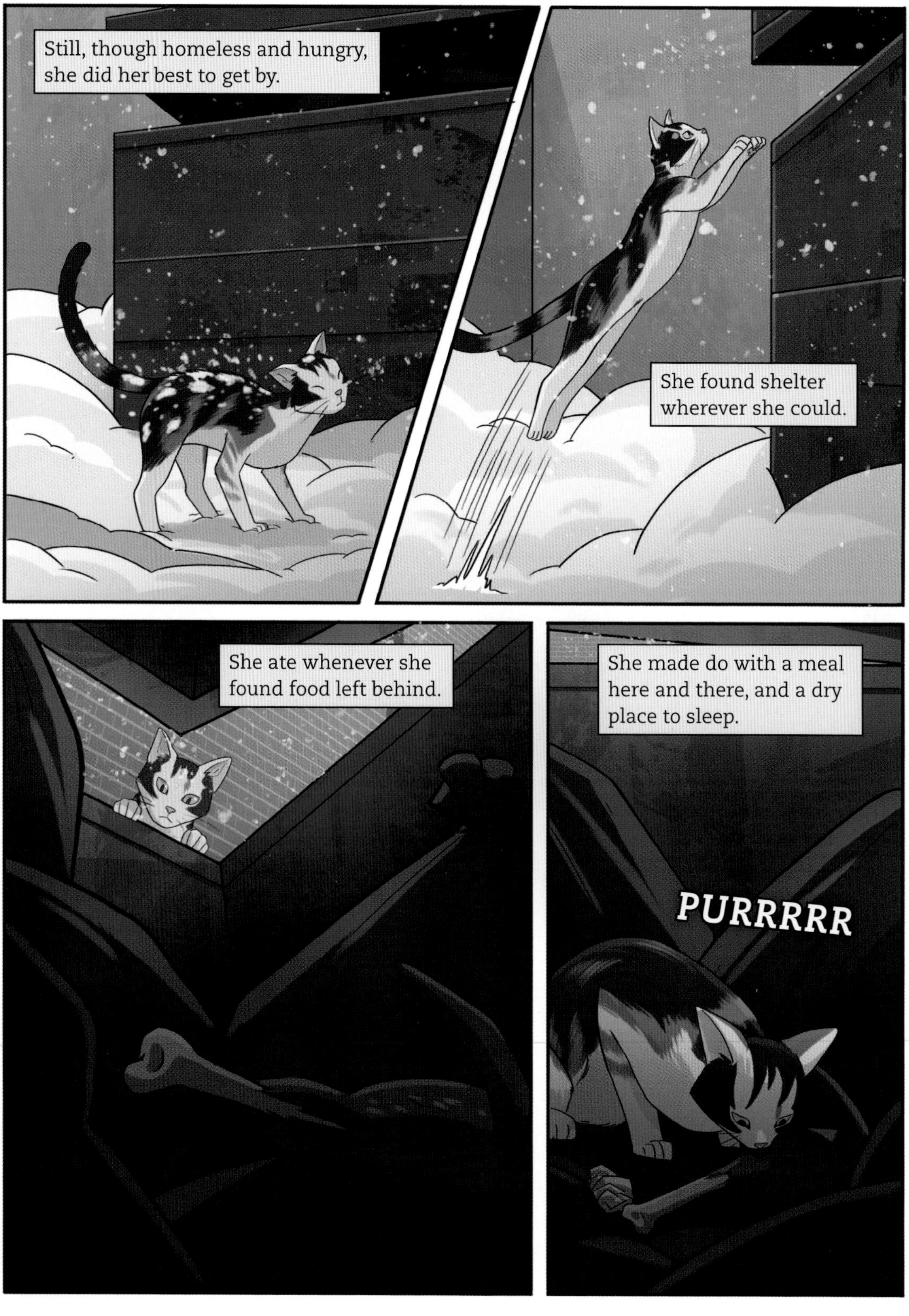
Still, though homeless and hungry, she did her best to get by.
She found shelter wherever she could.
She ate whenever she found food left behind.
She made do with a meal here and there, and a dry place to sleep.
PURRRRR

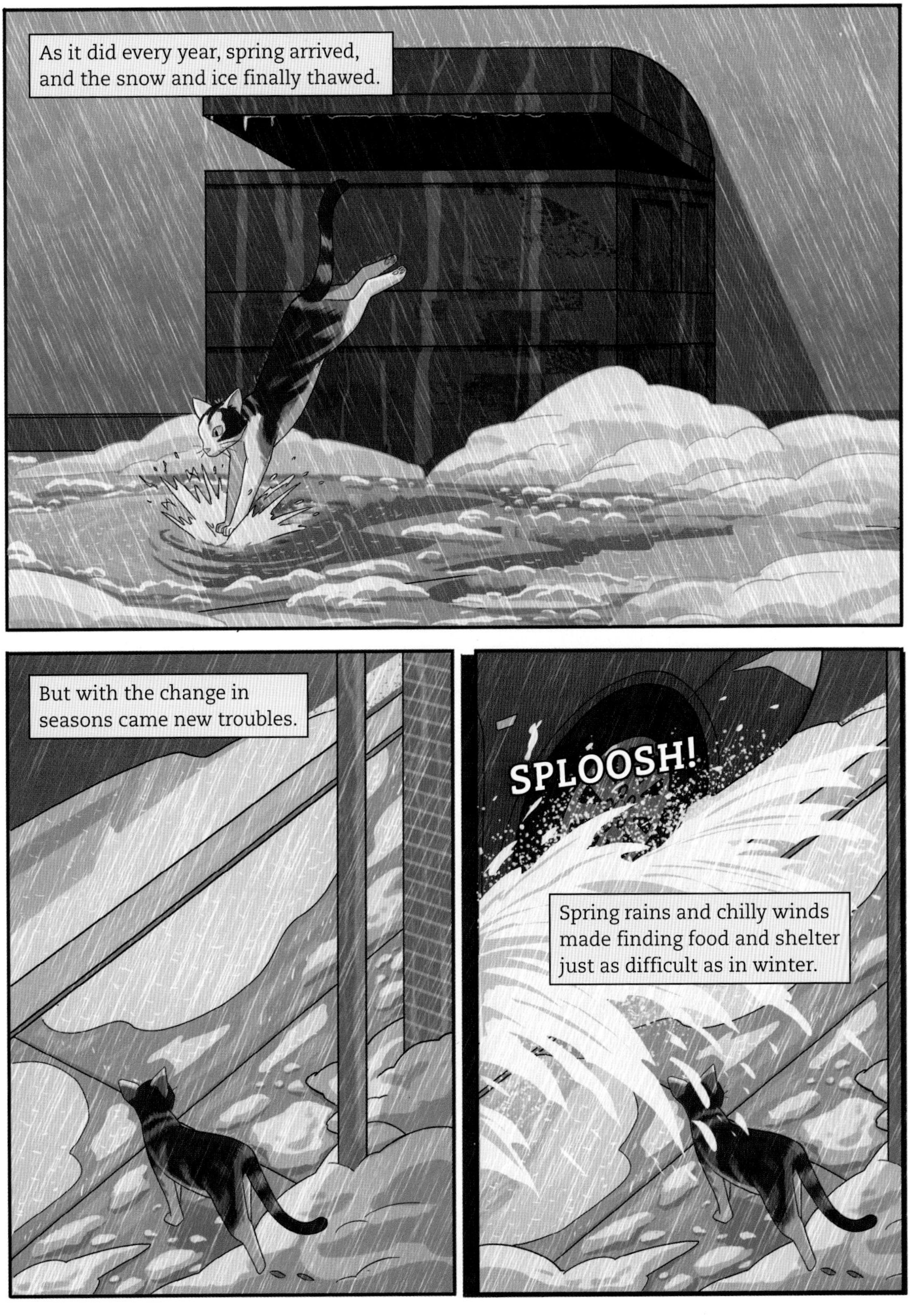
As it did every year, spring arrived, and the snow and ice finally thawed.
But with the change in seasons came new troubles.
SPLOOSH!
Spring rains and chilly winds made finding food and shelter just as difficult as in winter.

# Chapter 2: A Winding Path

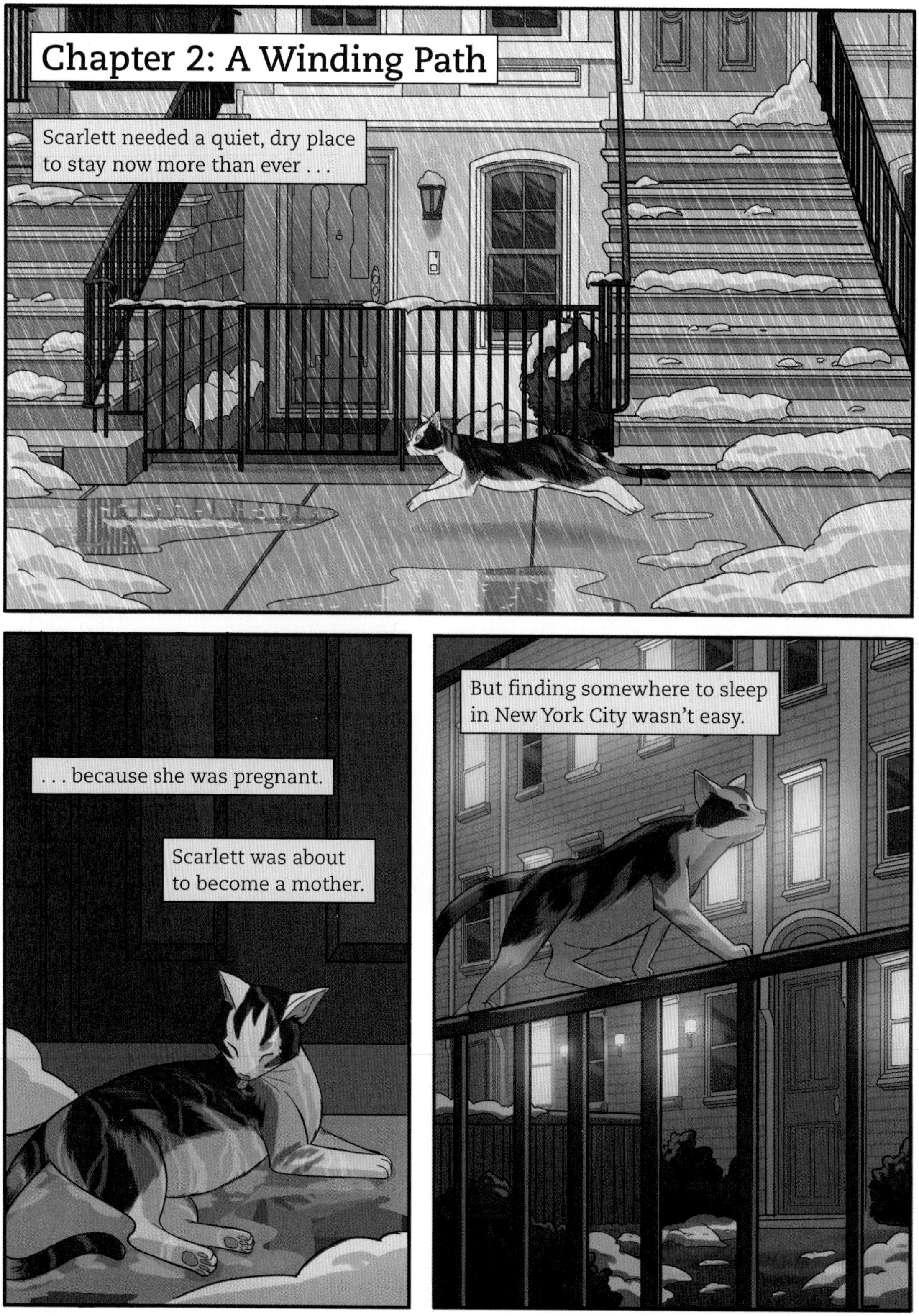
Scarlett needed a quiet, dry place to stay now more than ever . . .
. . . because she was pregnant.
Scarlett was about to become a mother.
But finding somewhere to sleep in New York City wasn't easy.

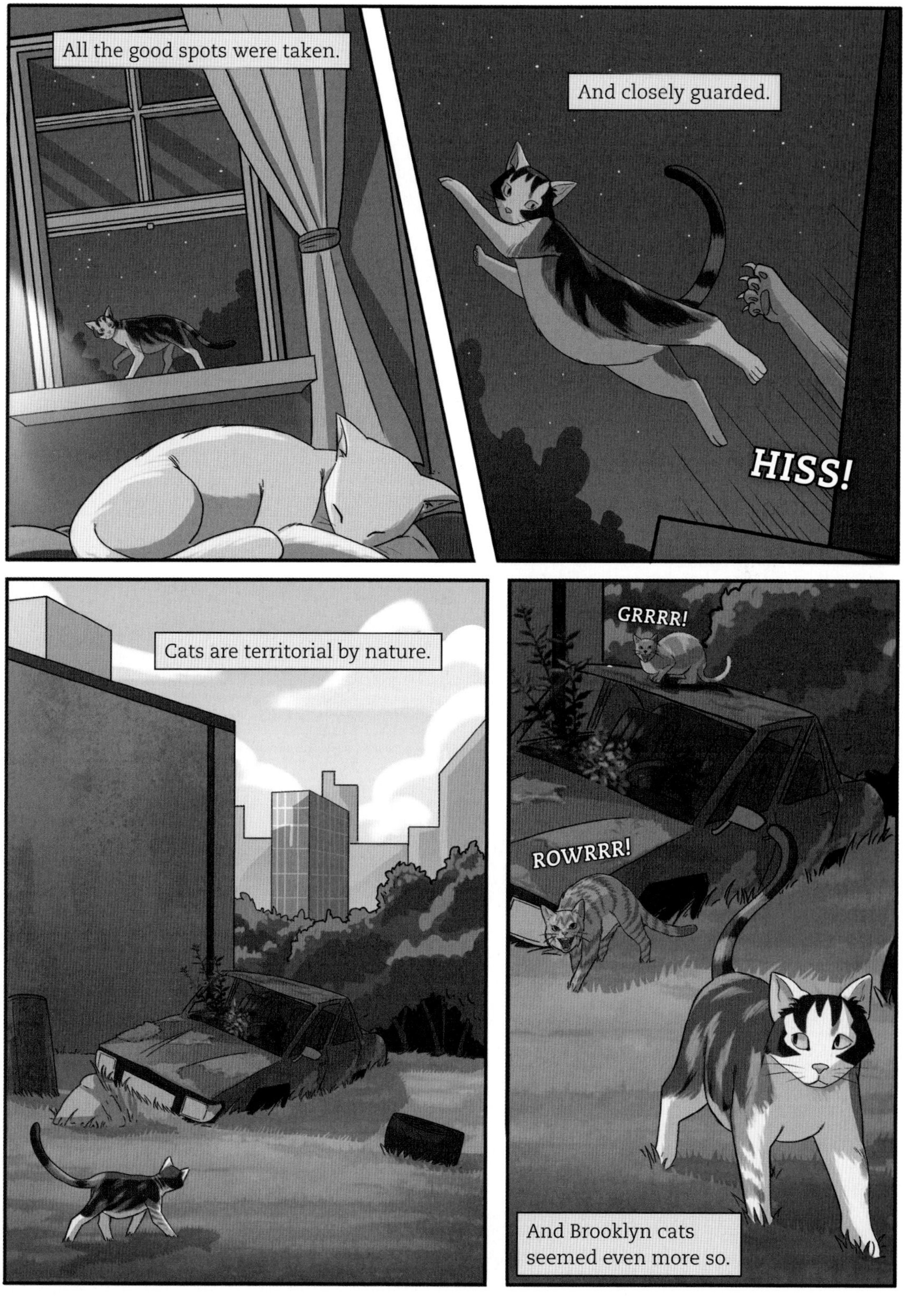
All the good spots were taken.
And closely guarded.
HISS!
Cats are territorial by nature.
GRRRR!
ROWRRR!
And Brooklyn cats
seemed even more so.

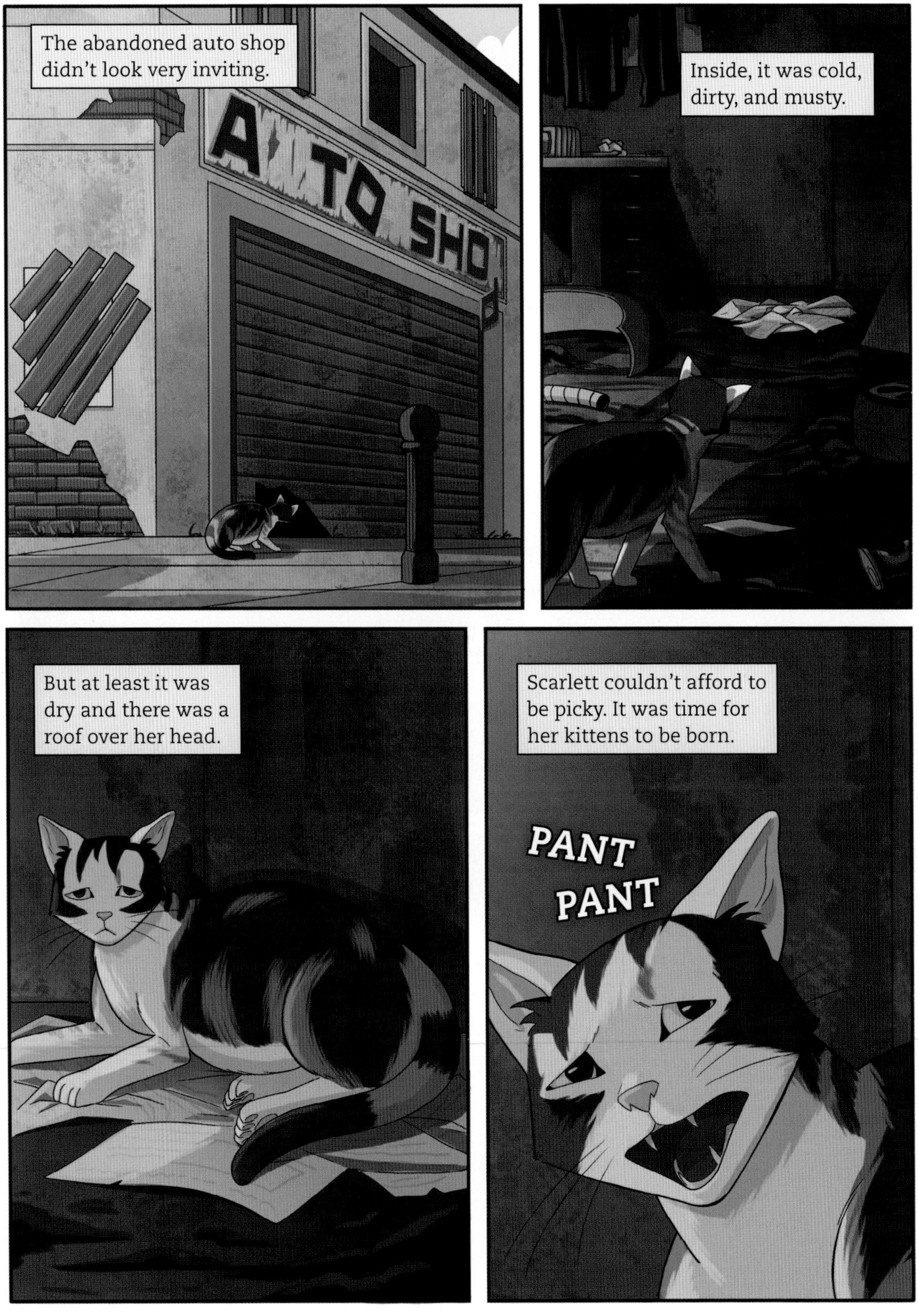
The abandoned auto shop didn't look very inviting.
A TO SHO
Inside, it was cold, dirty, and musty.
But at least it was dry and there was a roof over her head.
Scarlett couldn't afford to be picky. It was time for her kittens to be born.
PANT
PANT

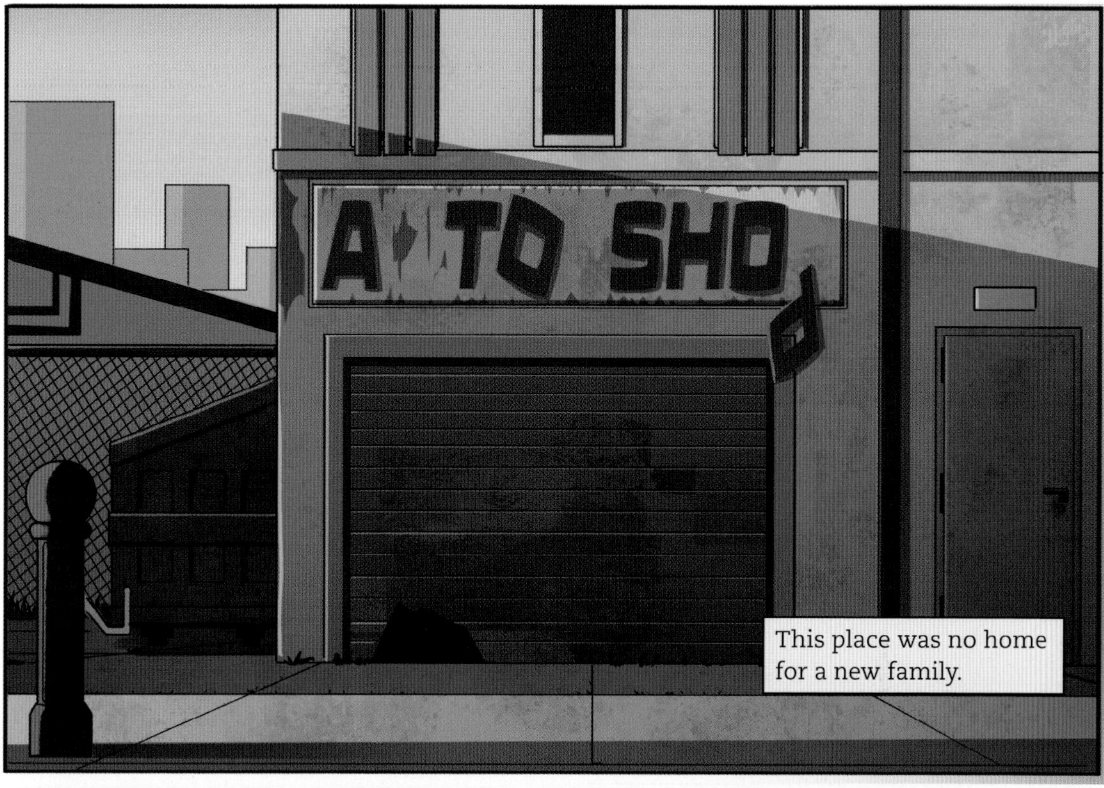
A TO SHO
This place was no home for a new family.

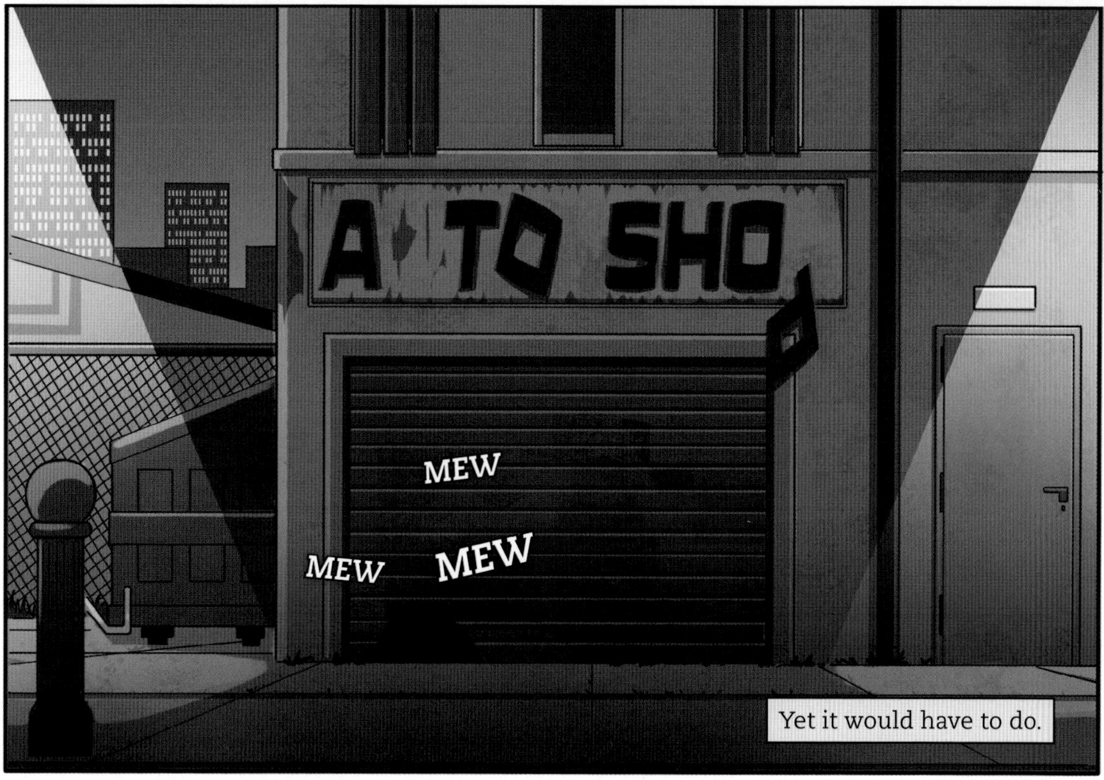
A TO SHO
MEW
MEW
MEW
Yet it would have to do.

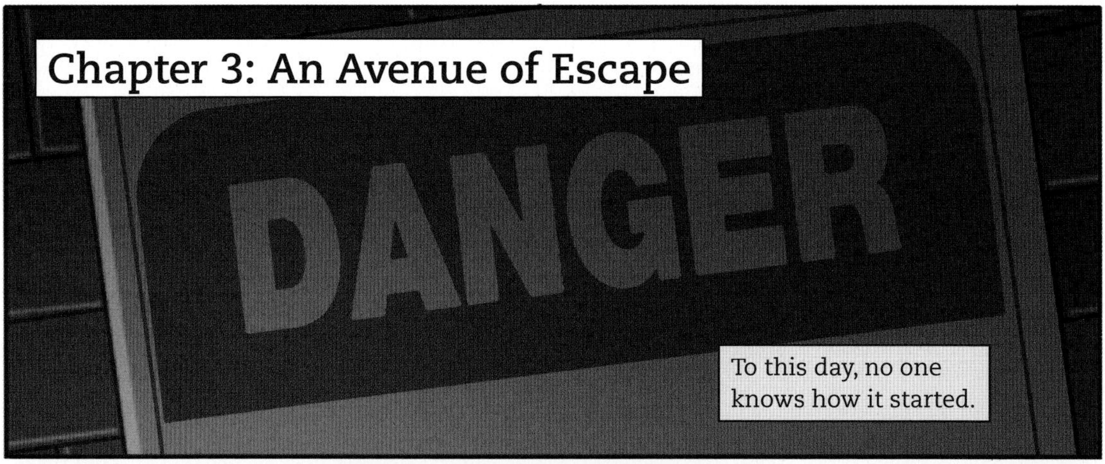
Chapter 3: An Avenue of Escape
DANGER
To this day, no one knows how it started.

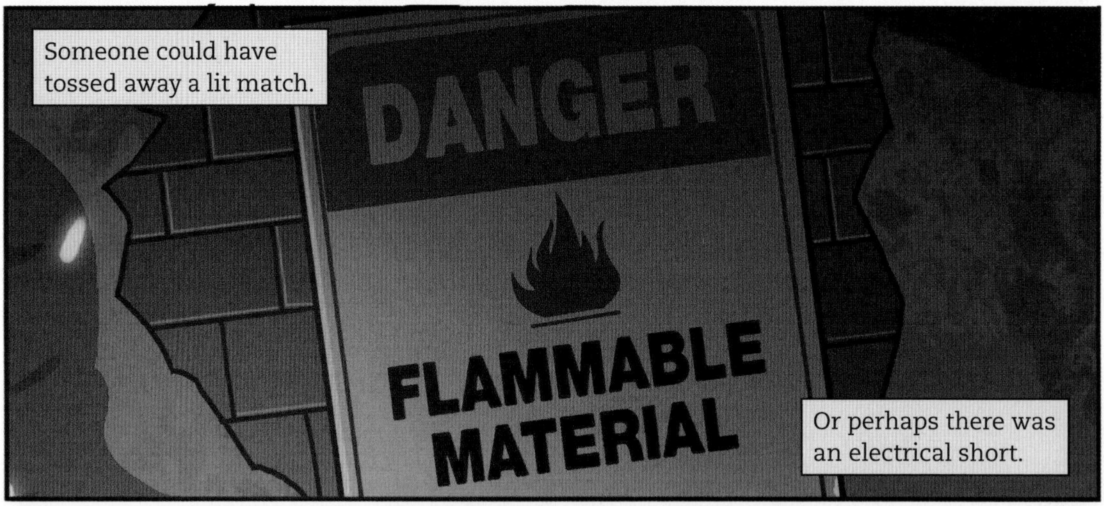
Someone could have tossed away a lit match.
DANGER
FLAMMABLE MATERIAL
Or perhaps there was an electrical short.

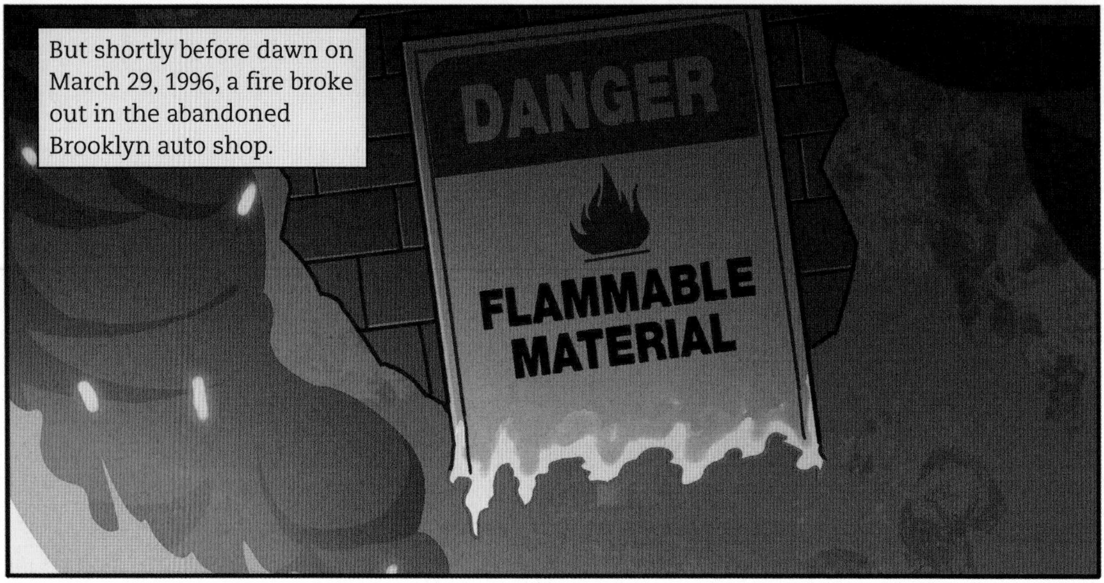
But shortly before dawn on March 29, 1996, a fire broke out in the abandoned Brooklyn auto shop.
DANGER
FLAMMABLE MATERIAL

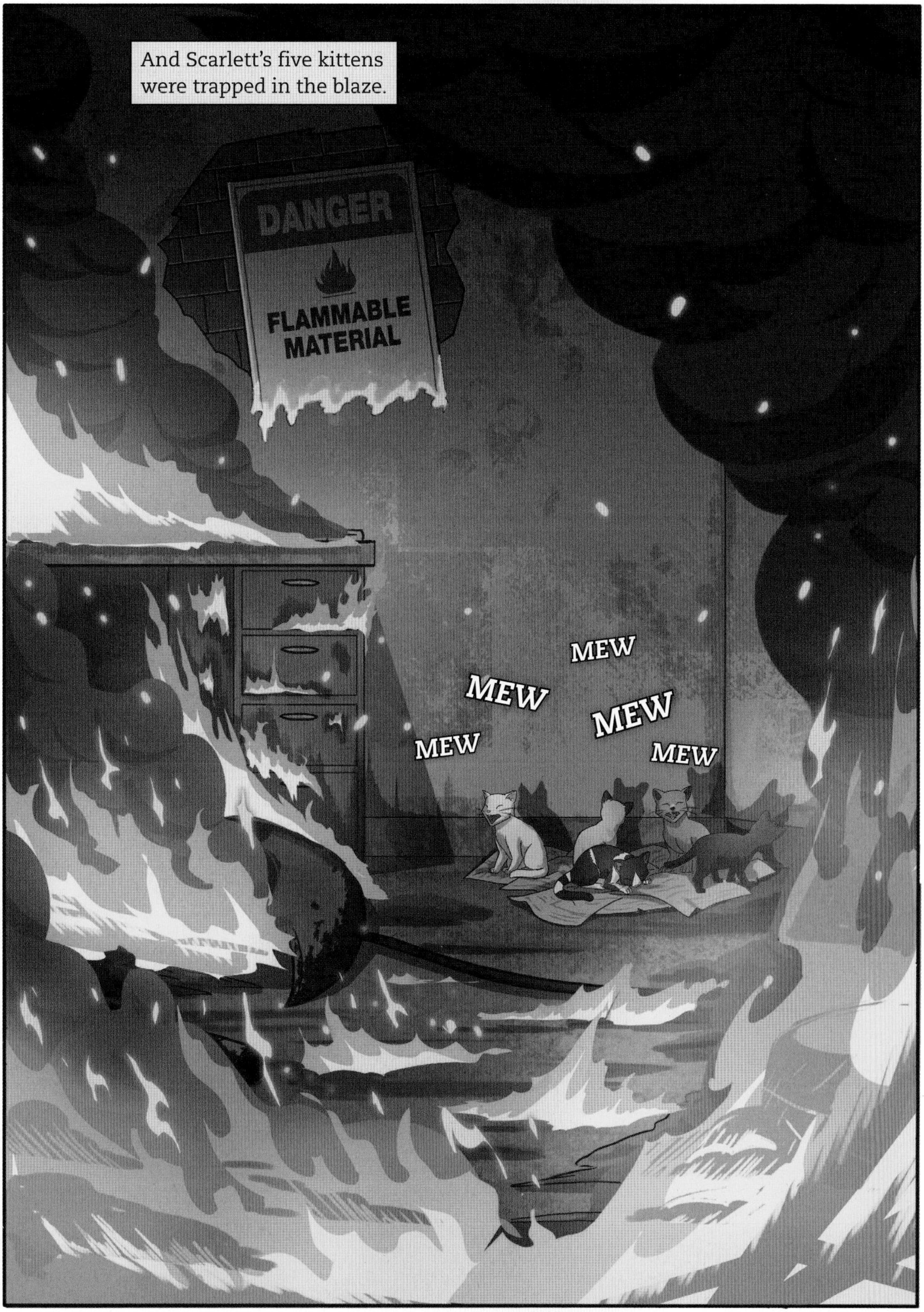
And Scarlett's five kittens were trapped in the blaze.
DANGER
FLAMMABLE MATERIAL
MEW
MEW
MEW
MEW
MEW

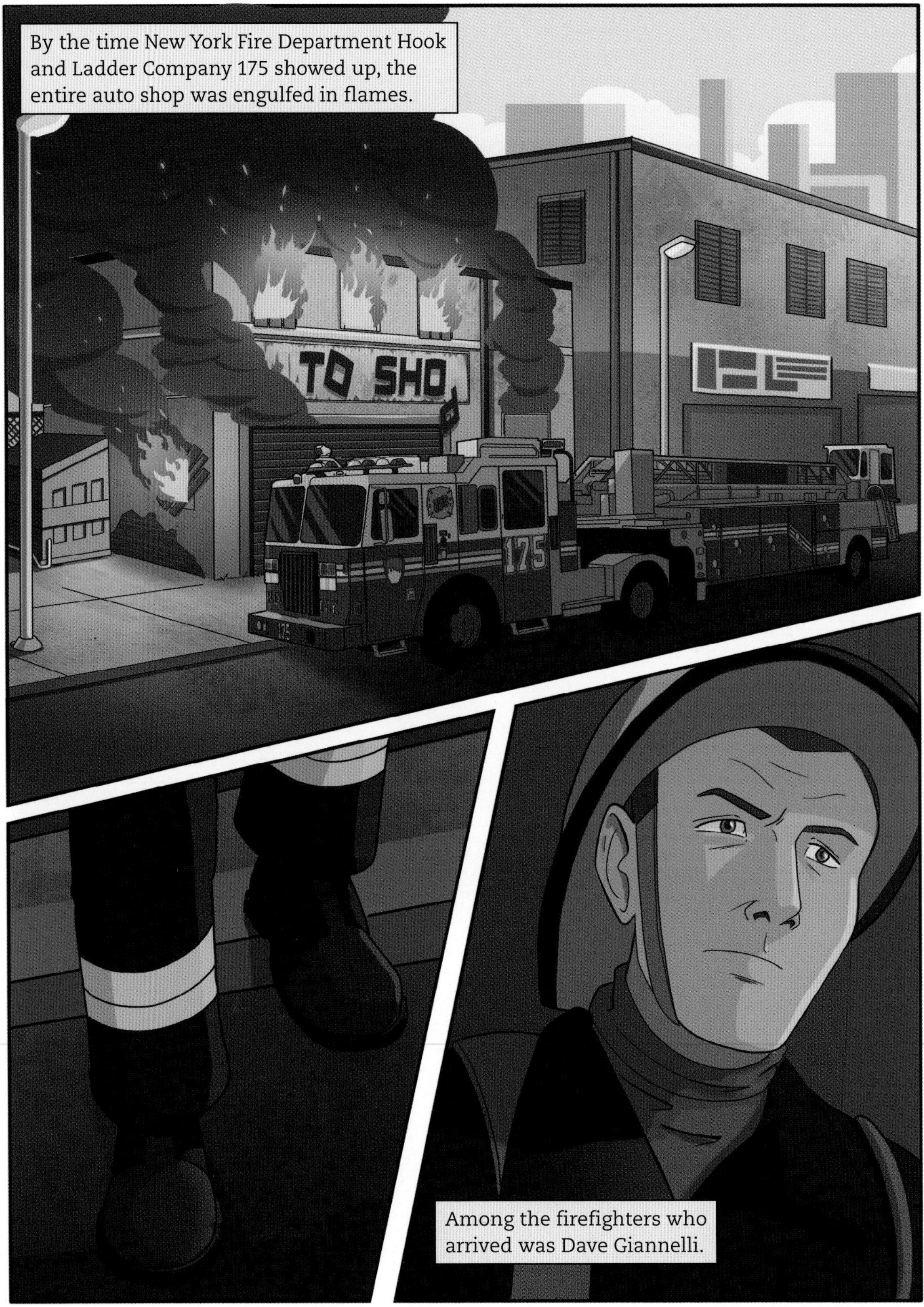
By the time New York Fire Department Hook and Ladder Company 175 showed up, the entire auto shop was engulfed in flames.
TO SHO
175
Among the firefighters who arrived was Dave Giannelli.

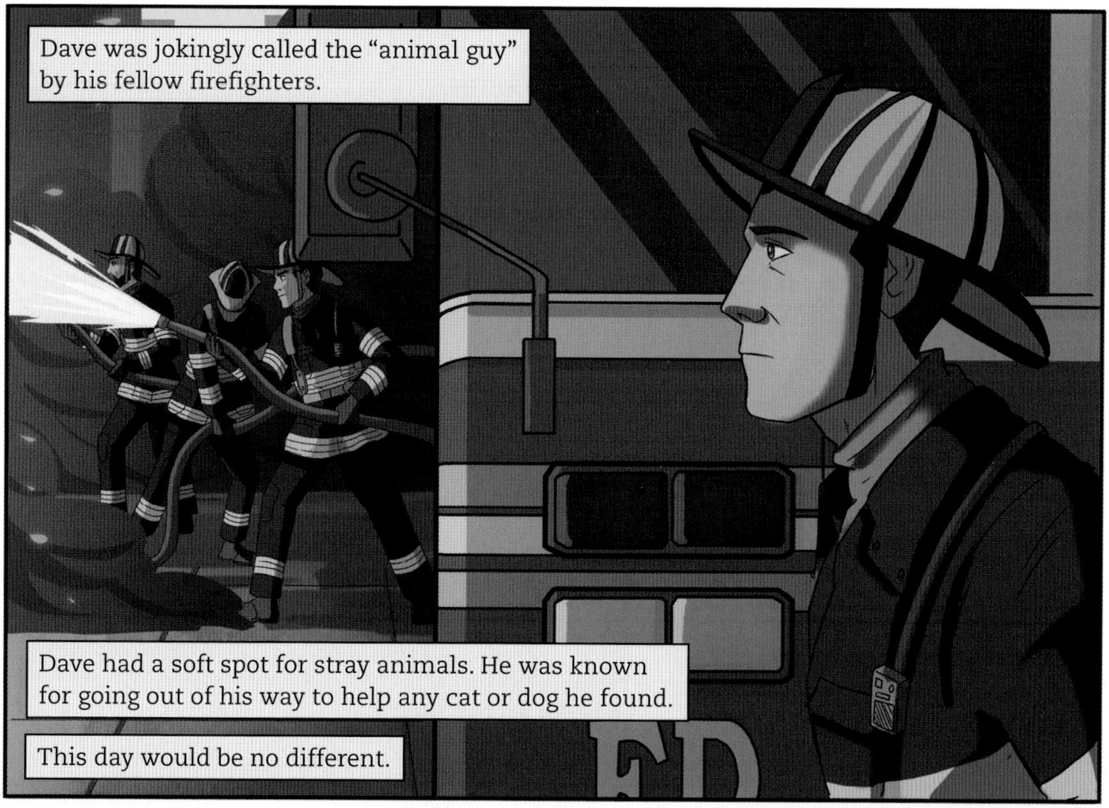
Dave was jokingly called the "animal guy" by his fellow firefighters.
Dave had a soft spot for stray animals. He was known for going out of his way to help any cat or dog he found.
This day would be no different.
FD

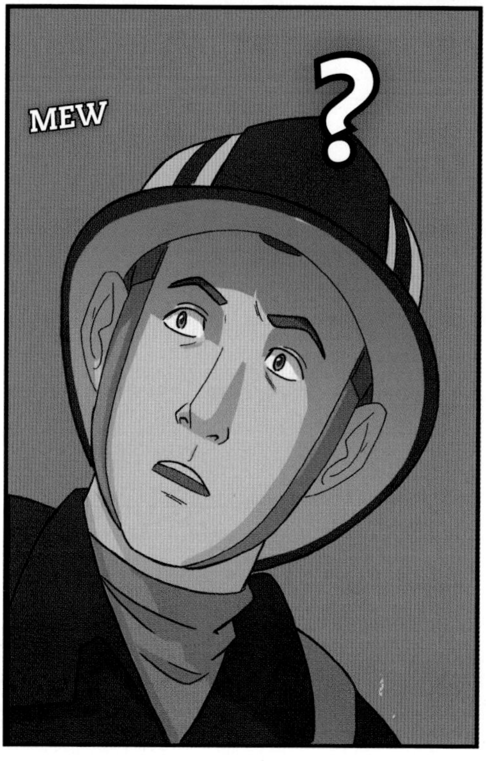
MEW
?

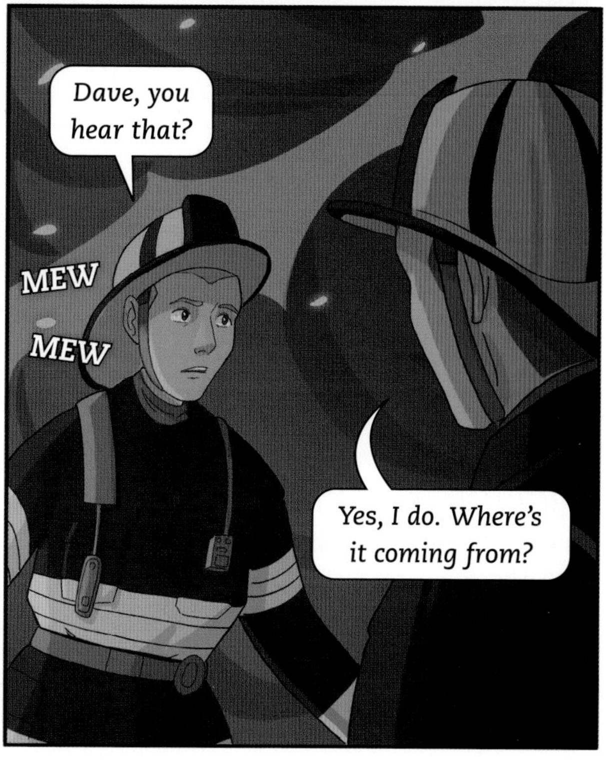
Dave, you hear that?
MEW
MEW
Yes, I do. Where's it coming from?

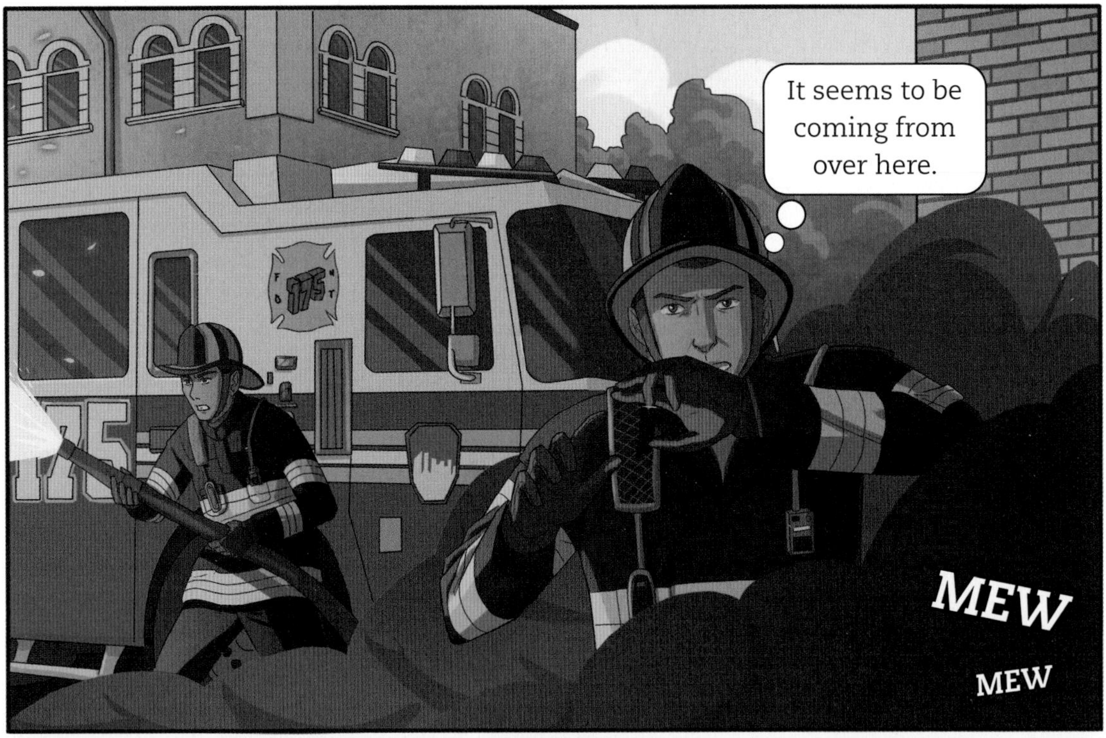
It seems to be coming from over here.
MEW
MEW

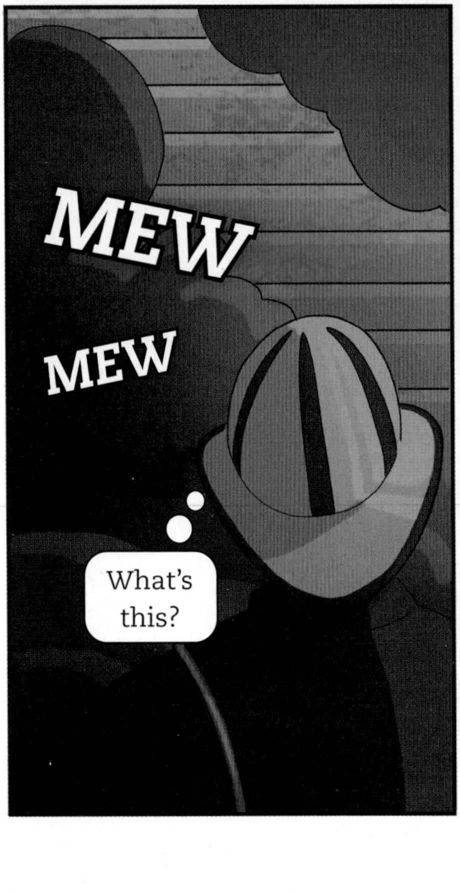
MEW
MEW
What's this?

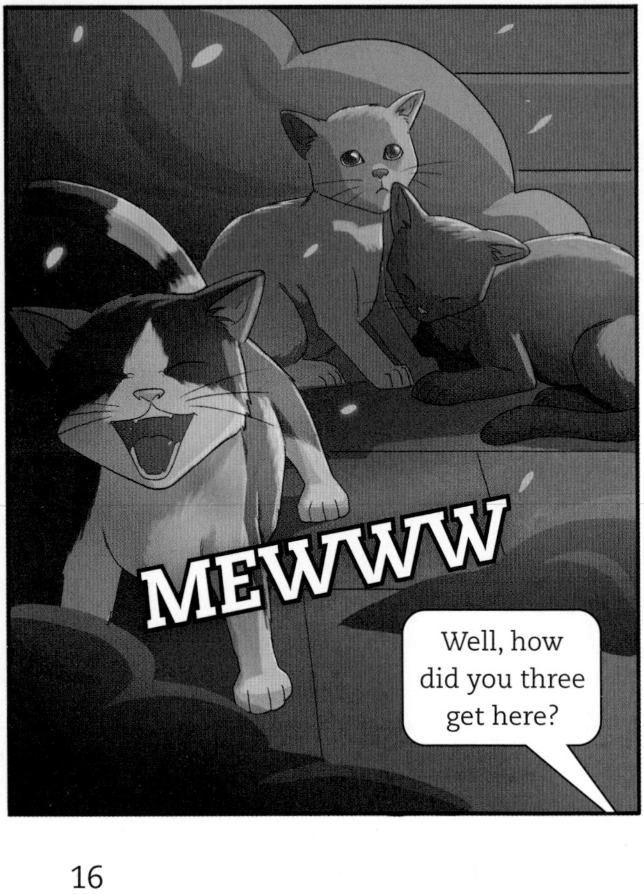
MEWWW
Well, how did you three get here?

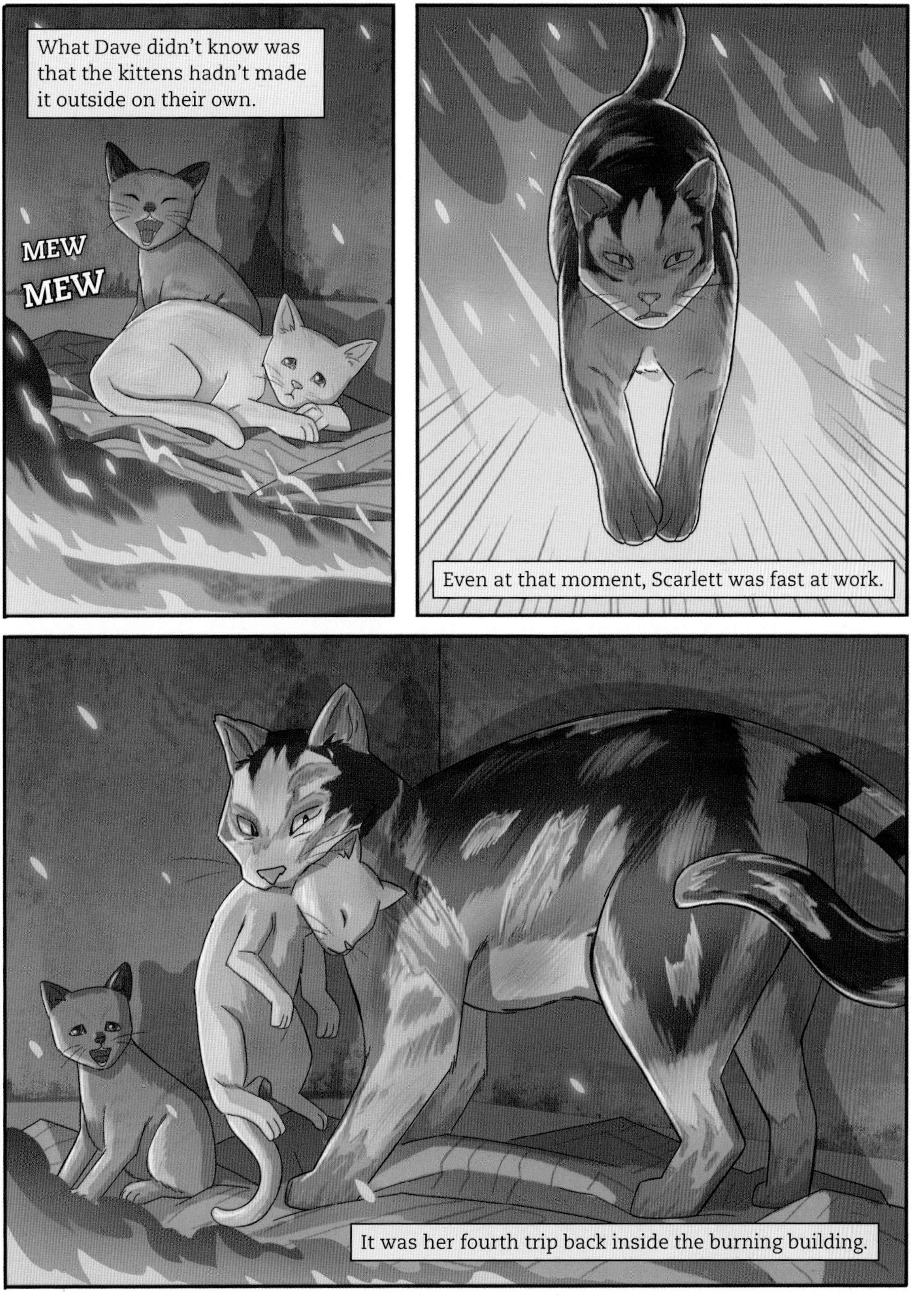

What Dave didn't know was that the kittens hadn't made it outside on their own.
MEW
MEW
Even at that moment, Scarlett was fast at work.
It was her fourth trip back inside the burning building.

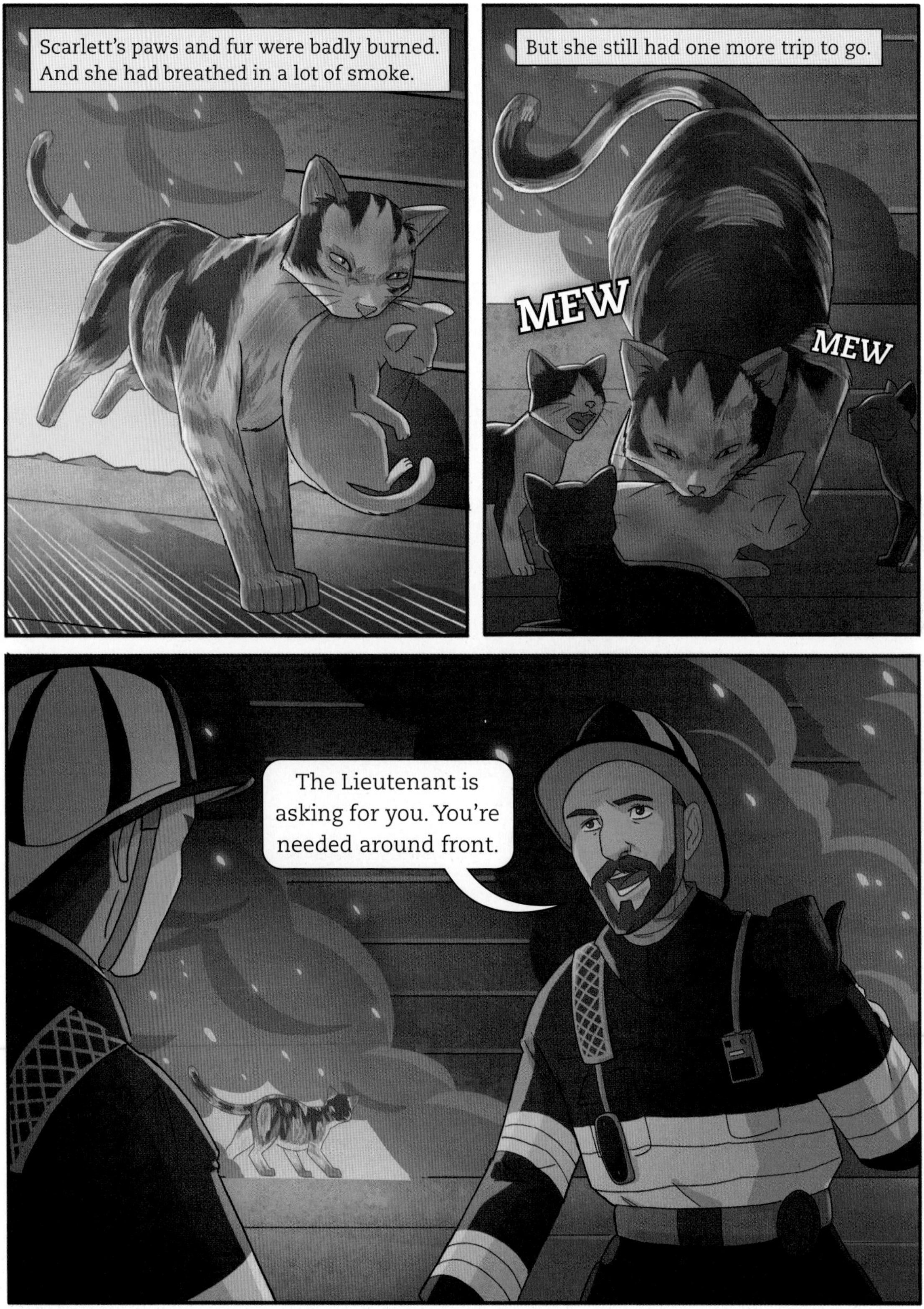
Scarlett's paws and fur were badly burned. And she had breathed in a lot of smoke.
But she still had one more trip to go.
MEW
MEW
The Lieutenant is asking for you. You're needed around front.

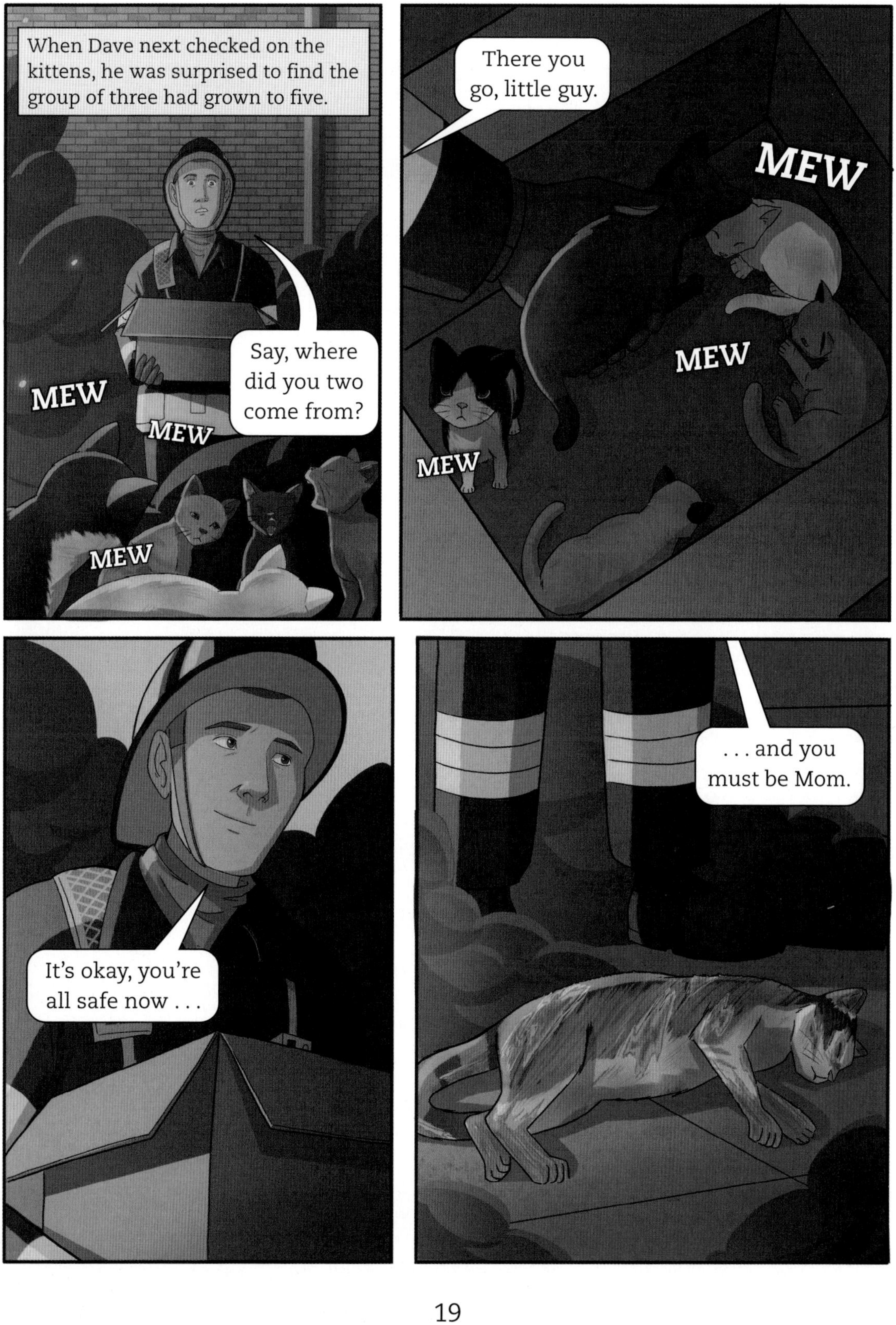

When Dave next checked on the kittens, he was surprised to find the group of three had grown to five.
Say, where did you two come from?
MEW
MEW
MEW
There you go, little guy.
MEW
MEW
MEW
It's okay, you're all safe now . . .
. . . and you must be Mom.

# Chapter 4: Road to Recovery

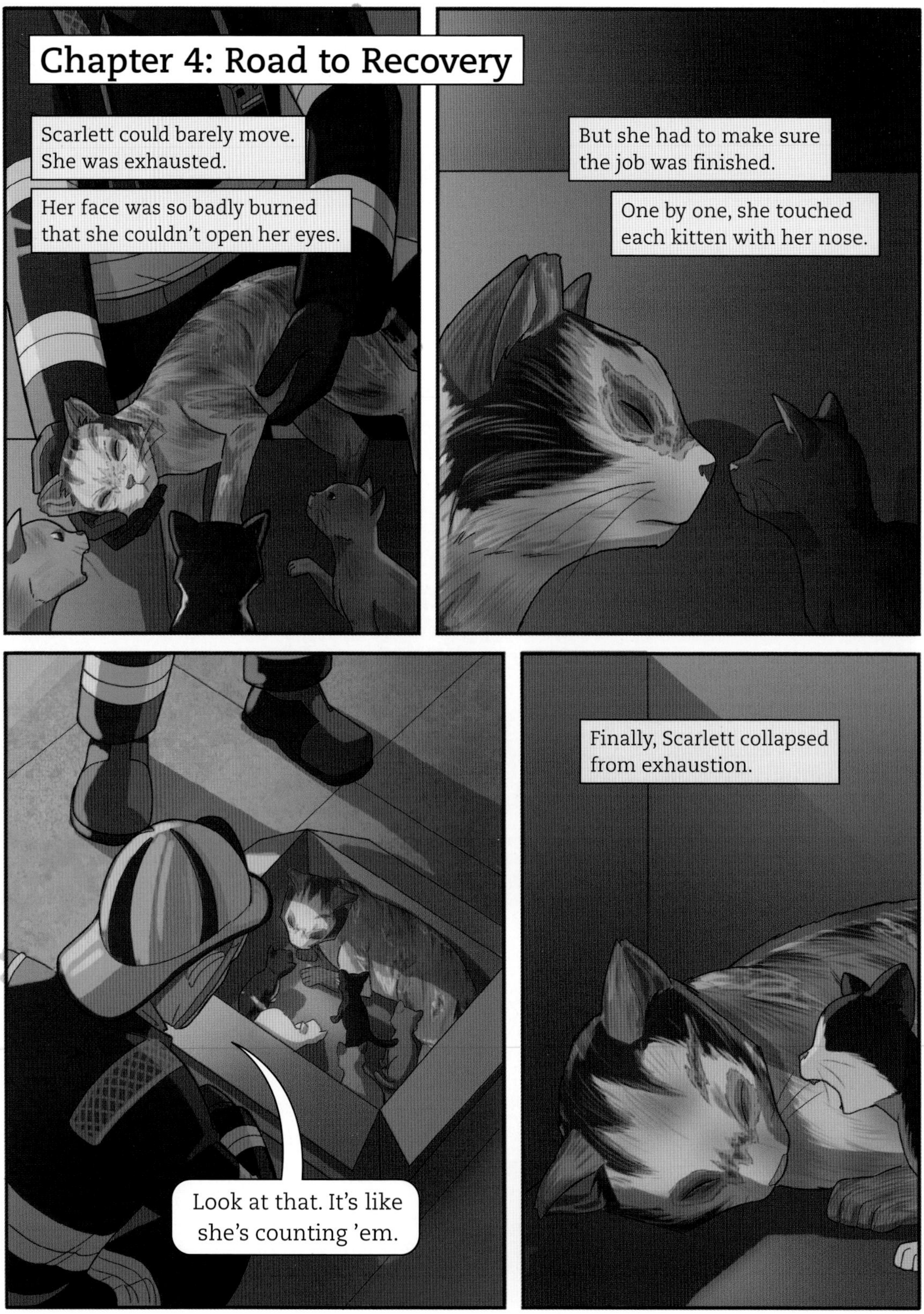
Scarlett could barely move. She was exhausted.
Her face was so badly burned that she couldn't open her eyes.
But she had to make sure the job was finished.
One by one, she touched each kitten with her nose.
Look at that. It's like she's counting 'em.
Finally, Scarlett collapsed from exhaustion.

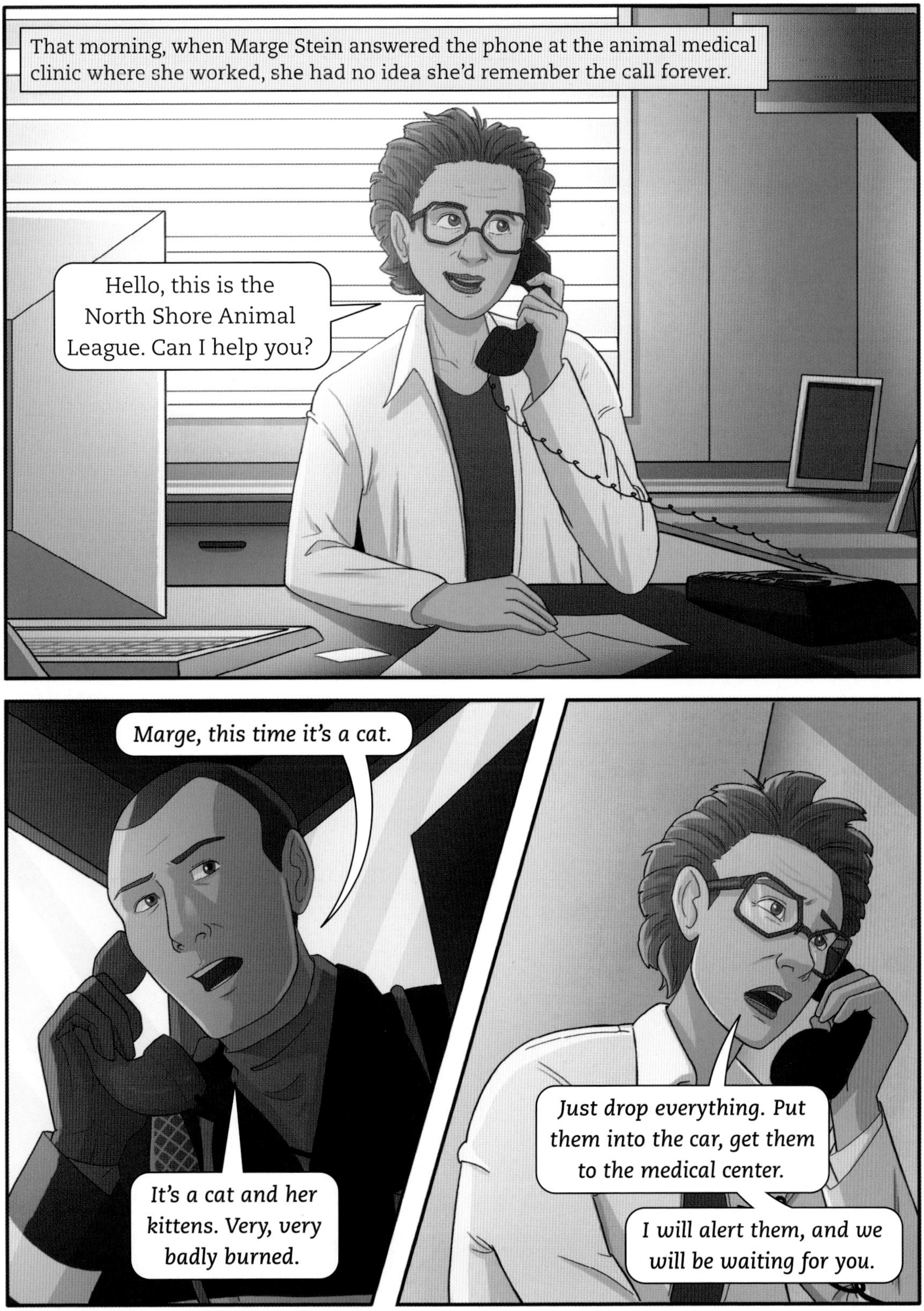
That morning, when Marge Stein answered the phone at the animal medical clinic where she worked, she had no idea she'd remember the call forever.
Hello, this is the North Shore Animal League. Can I help you?
Marge, this time it's a cat.
It's a cat and her kittens. Very, very badly burned.
Just drop everything. Put them into the car, get them to the medical center.
I will alert them, and we will be waiting for you.

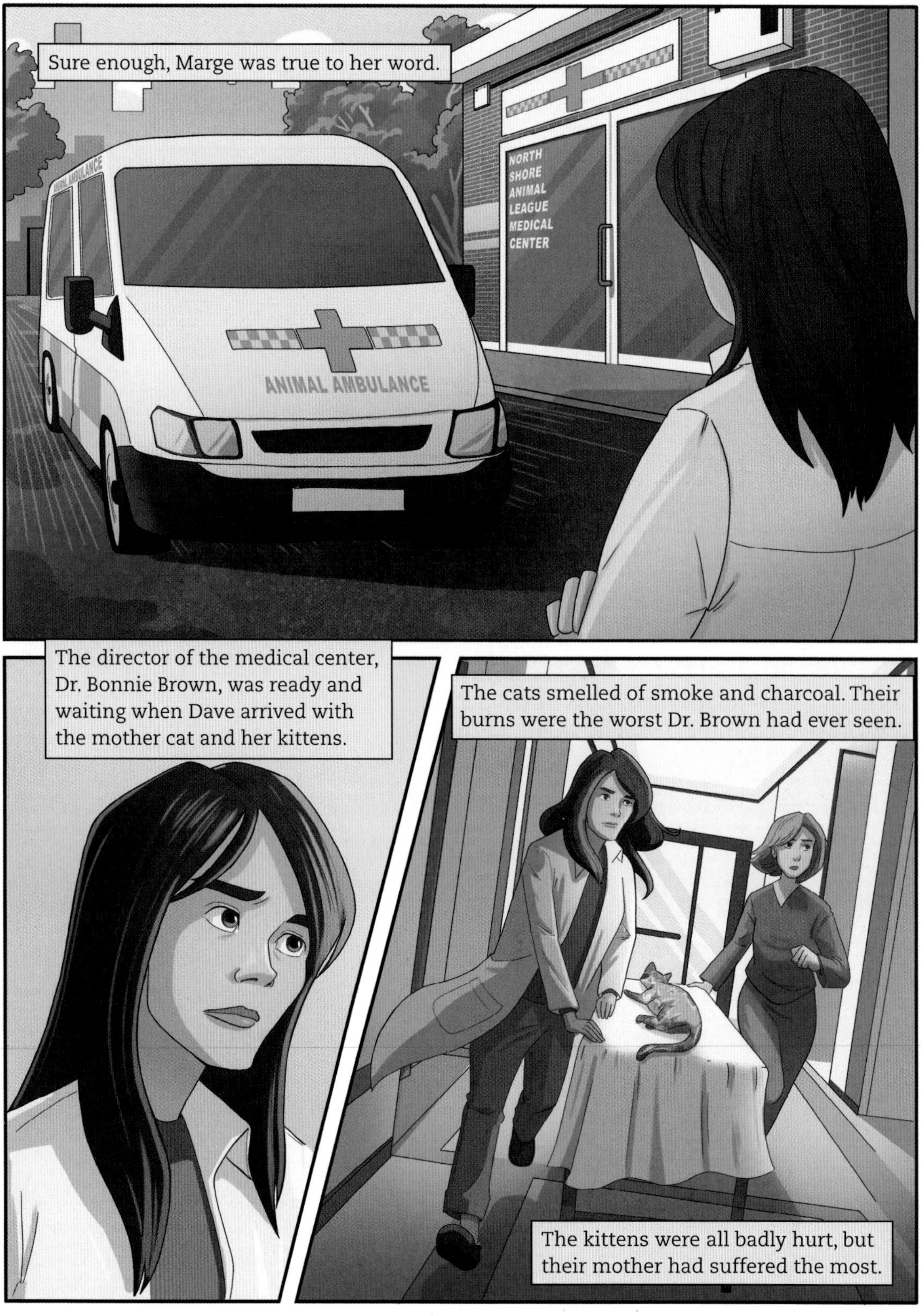
Sure enough, Marge was true to her word.
NORTH SHORE ANIMAL LEAGUE MEDICAL CENTER
ANIMAL AMBULANCE
ANIMAL AMBULANCE
The director of the medical center, Dr. Bonnie Brown, was ready and waiting when Dave arrived with the mother cat and her kittens.
The cats smelled of smoke and charcoal. Their burns were the worst Dr. Brown had ever seen.
The kittens were all badly hurt, but their mother had suffered the most.

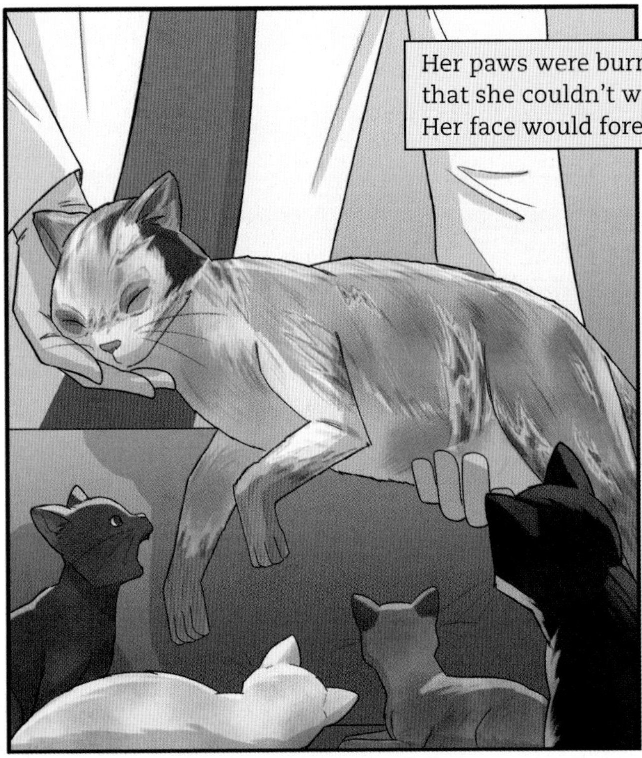
Her paws were burned so badly that she couldn't walk on them. Her face would forever be scarred.

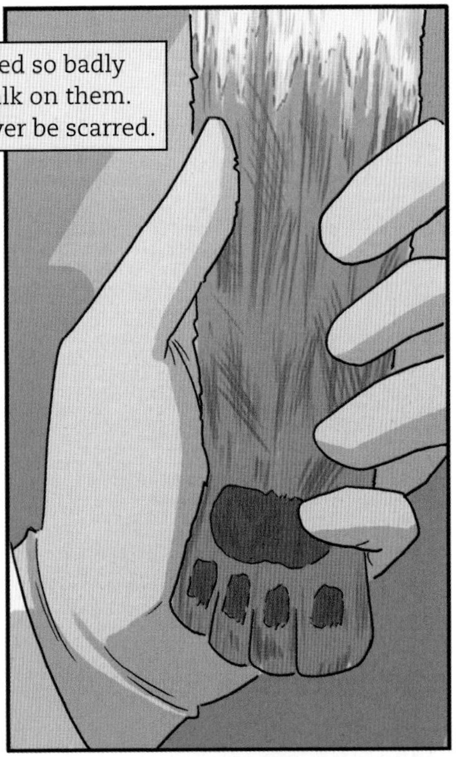

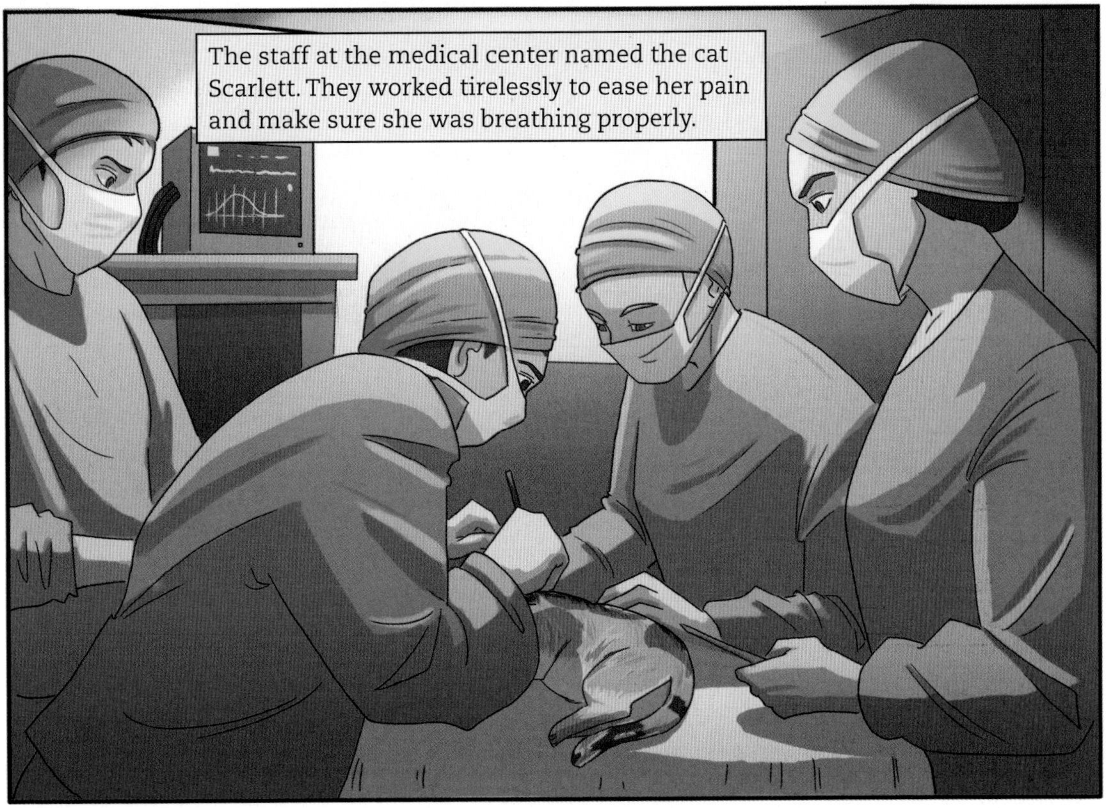
The staff at the medical center named the cat Scarlett. They worked tirelessly to ease her pain and make sure she was breathing properly.

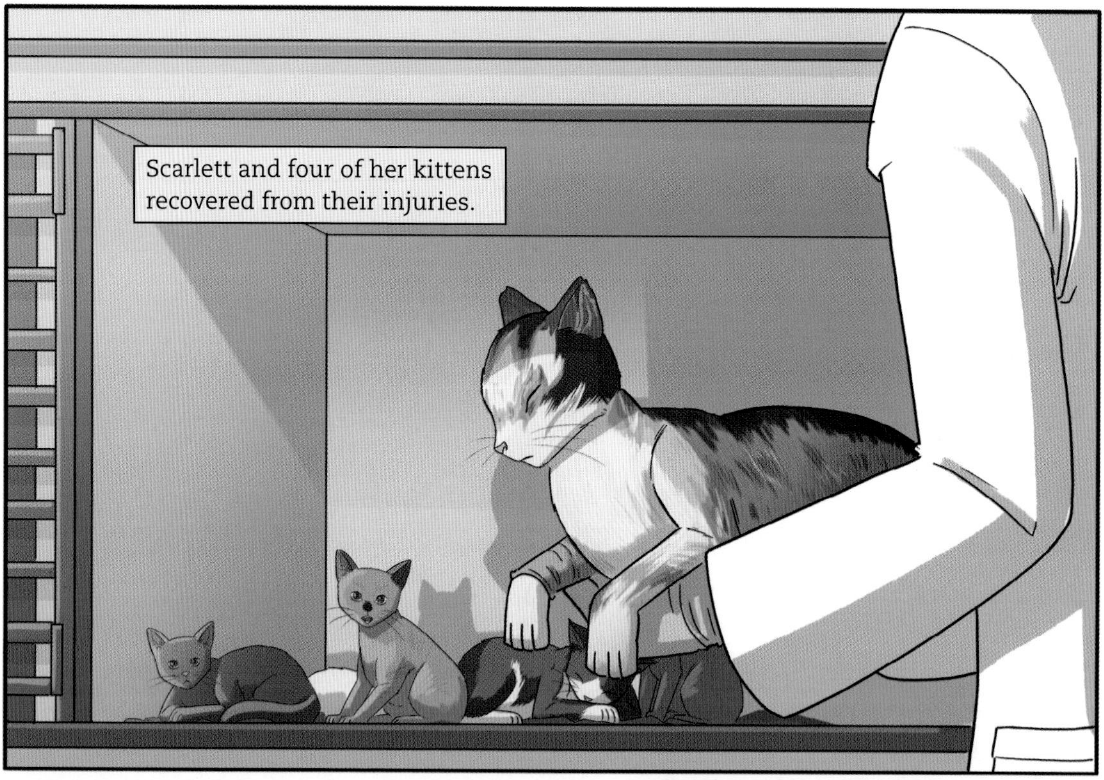
Scarlett and four of her kittens recovered from their injuries.

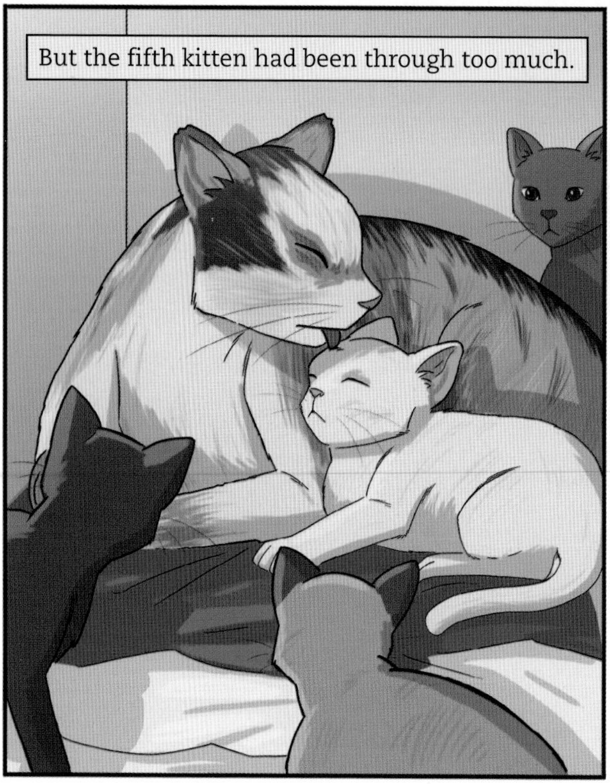
But the fifth kitten had been through too much.

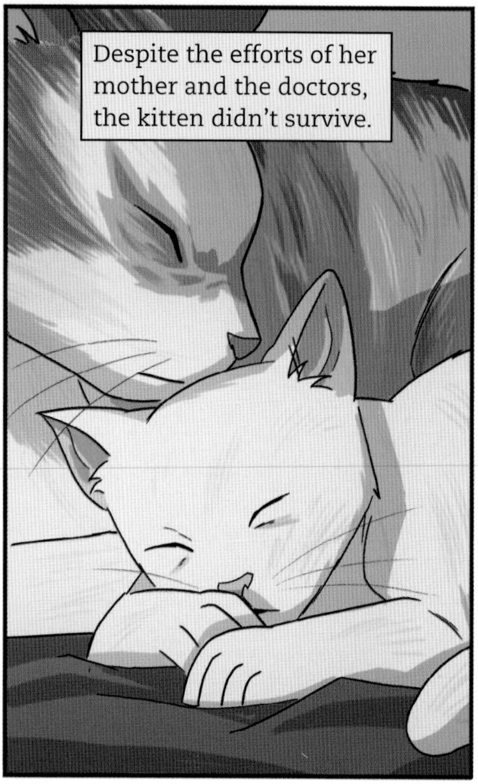
Despite the efforts of her mother and the doctors, the kitten didn't survive.

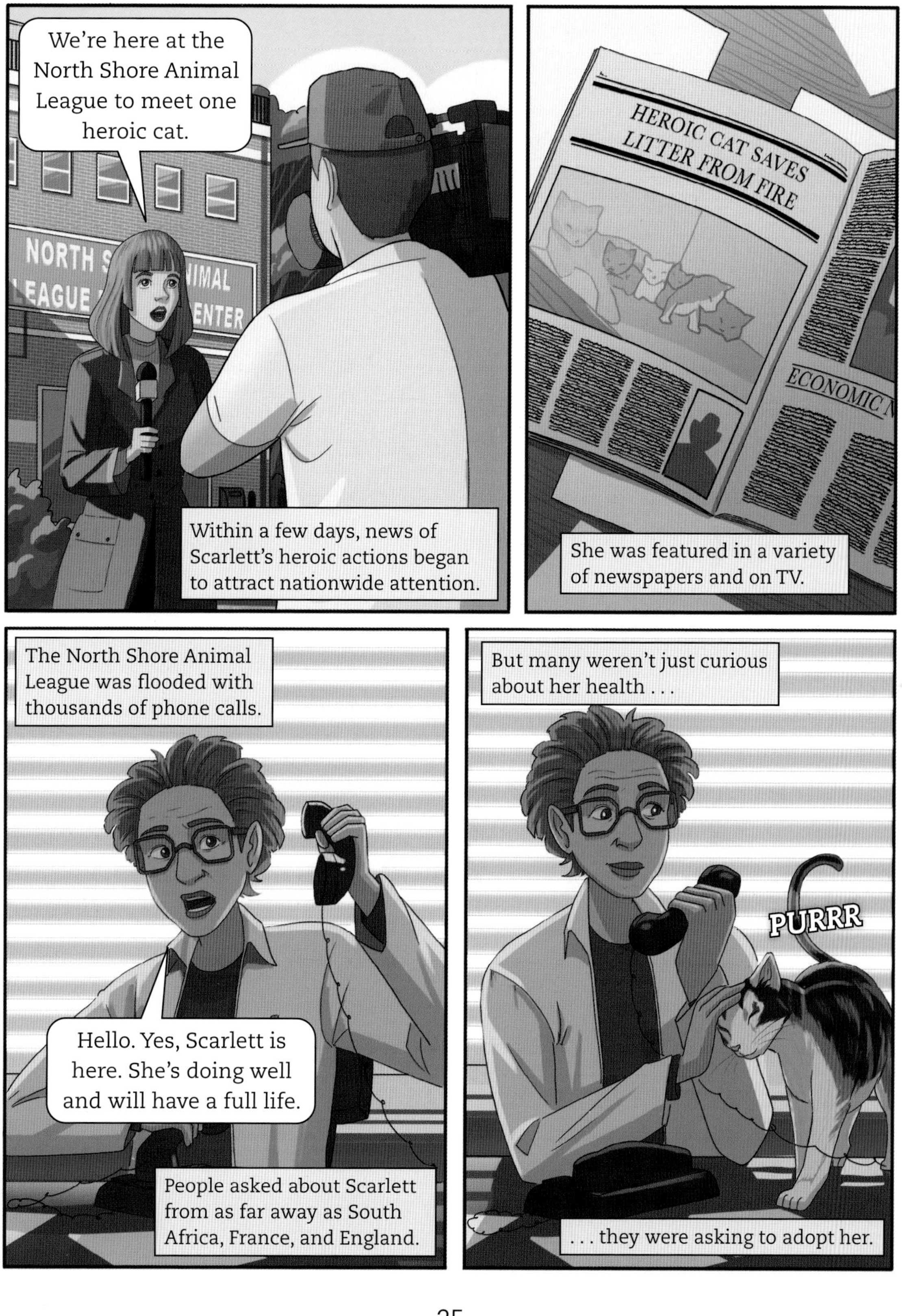
We're here at the North Shore Animal League to meet one heroic cat.
Within a few days, news of Scarlett's heroic actions began to attract nationwide attention.
HEROIC CAT SAVES LITTER FROM FIRE
She was featured in a variety of newspapers and on TV.
The North Shore Animal League was flooded with thousands of phone calls.
Hello. Yes, Scarlett is here. She's doing well and will have a full life.
People asked about Scarlett from as far away as South Africa, France, and England.
But many weren't just curious about her health . . .
PURRR
. . . they were asking to adopt her.

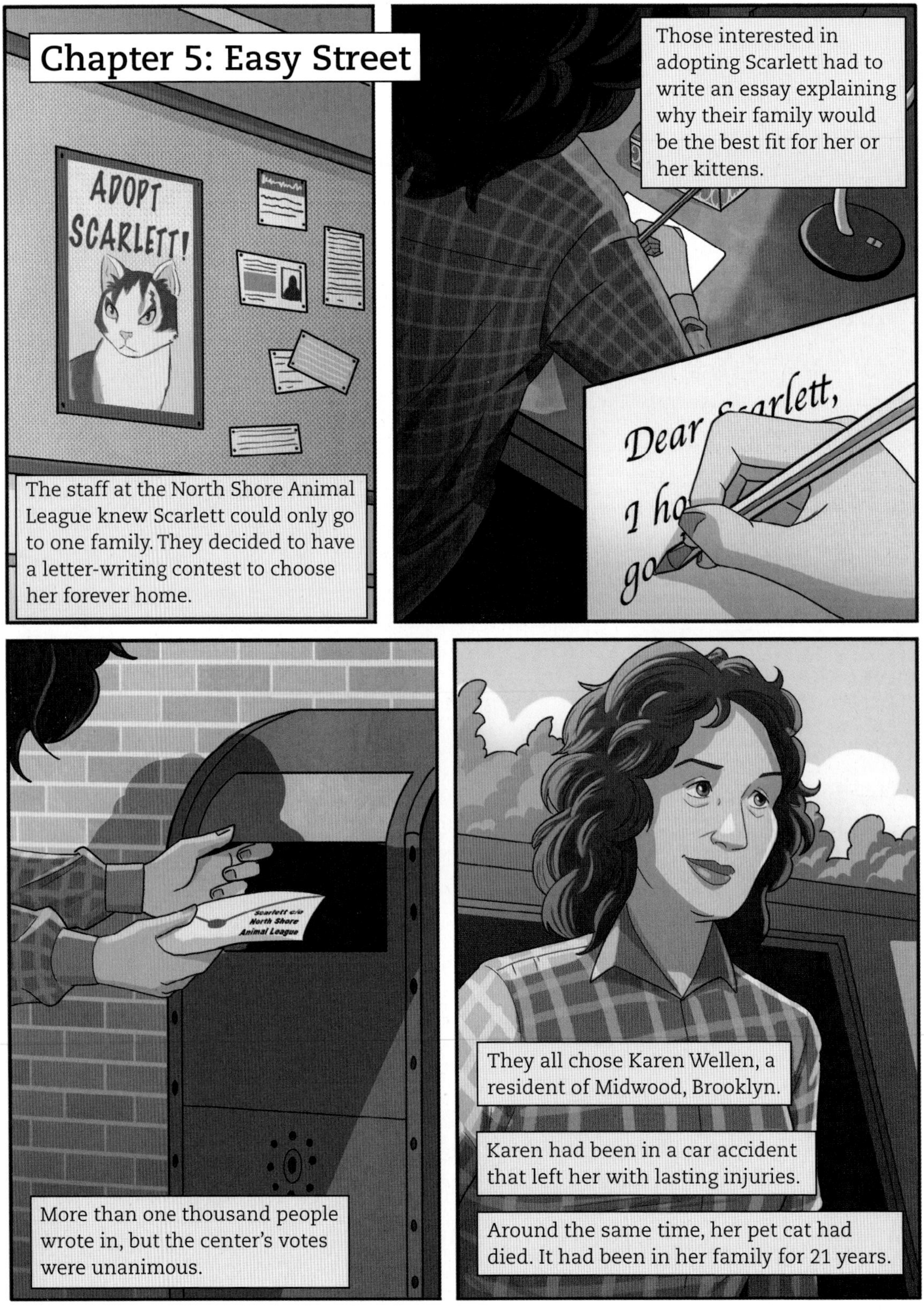
Chapter 5: Easy Street
ADOPT SCARLETT!
The staff at the North Shore Animal League knew Scarlett could only go to one family. They decided to have a letter-writing contest to choose her forever home.
Those interested in adopting Scarlett had to write an essay explaining why their family would be the best fit for her or her kittens.
Scarlett c/o North Shore Animal League
More than one thousand people wrote in, but the center's votes were unanimous.
They all chose Karen Wellen, a resident of Midwood, Brooklyn.
Karen had been in a car accident that left her with lasting injuries.
Around the same time, her pet cat had died. It had been in her family for 21 years.

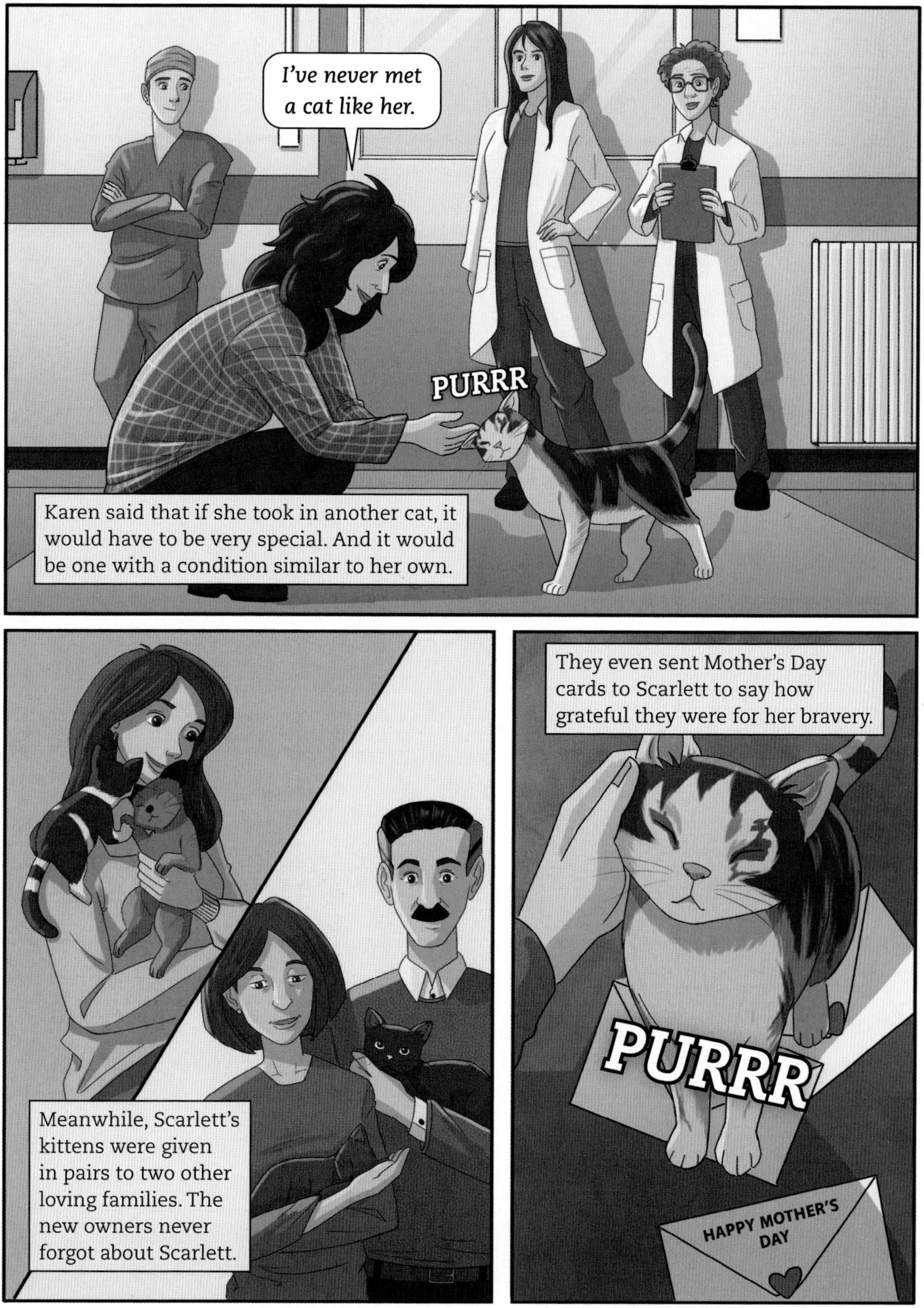
I've never met a cat like her.
PURRR
Karen said that if she took in another cat, it would have to be very special. And it would be one with a condition similar to her own.
Meanwhile, Scarlett's kittens were given in pairs to two other loving families. The new owners never forgot about Scarlett.
They even sent Mother's Day cards to Scarlett to say how grateful they were for her bravery.
PURRR
HAPPY MOTHER'S DAY

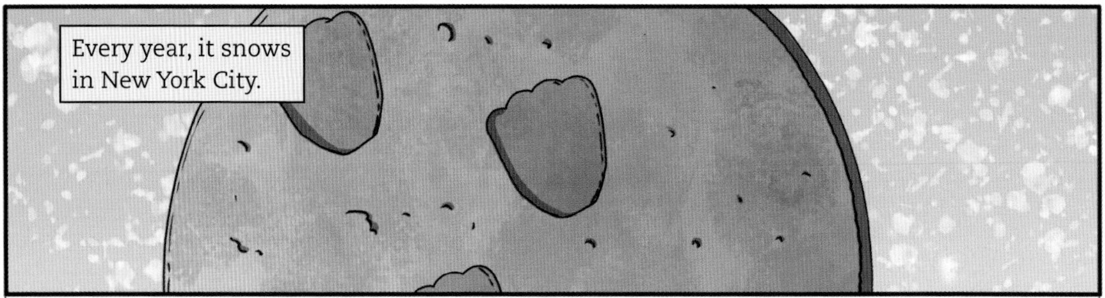
Every year, it snows in New York City.
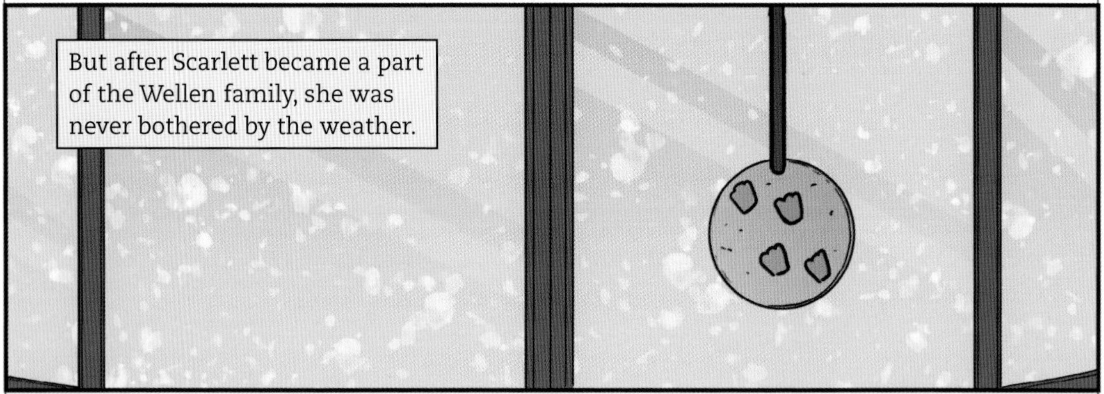
But after Scarlett became a part of the Wellen family, she was never bothered by the weather.
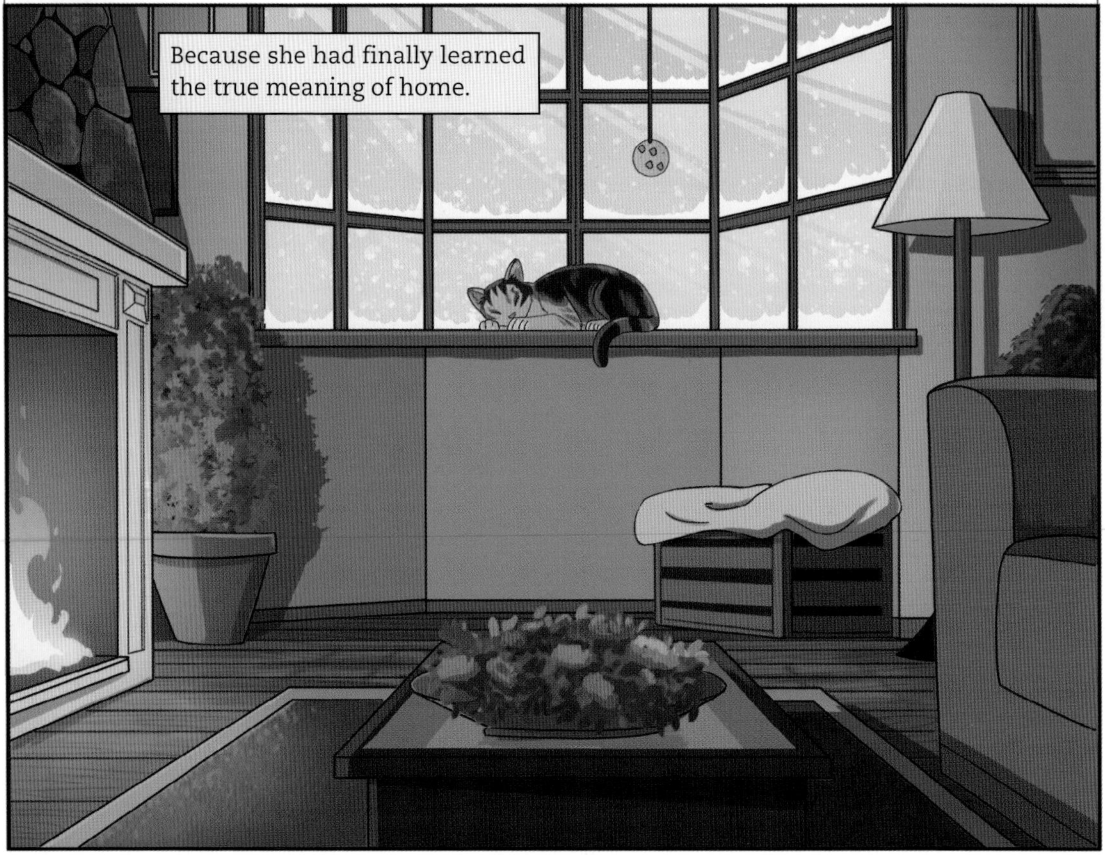
Because she had finally learned the true meaning of home.

# Scarlett's Story

Thanks to the North Shore Animal League and Karen Wellen, Scarlett made a full recovery. Her eyes were damaged and required daily drops, and her ears had to be clipped. But she healed quickly and soon put on weight.

In fact, Scarlett was spoiled endlessly by the Wellen family. She was fed well and given constant attention. She died on October 11, 2008. It's believed she was 13 years old. That would be 68 in human years!

Throughout her life, Scarlett had been featured on a variety of TV shows from "Inside Edition" to "Reading Rainbow." She starred in several books and received a certificate of bravery from the British Royal Society for the Prevention of Cruelty to Animals. She even had an award named after her: the Scarlett Award for Animal Heroism. While the tale of her bravery remains her legacy to the world, Scarlett will always be remembered most fondly by her adopted family.

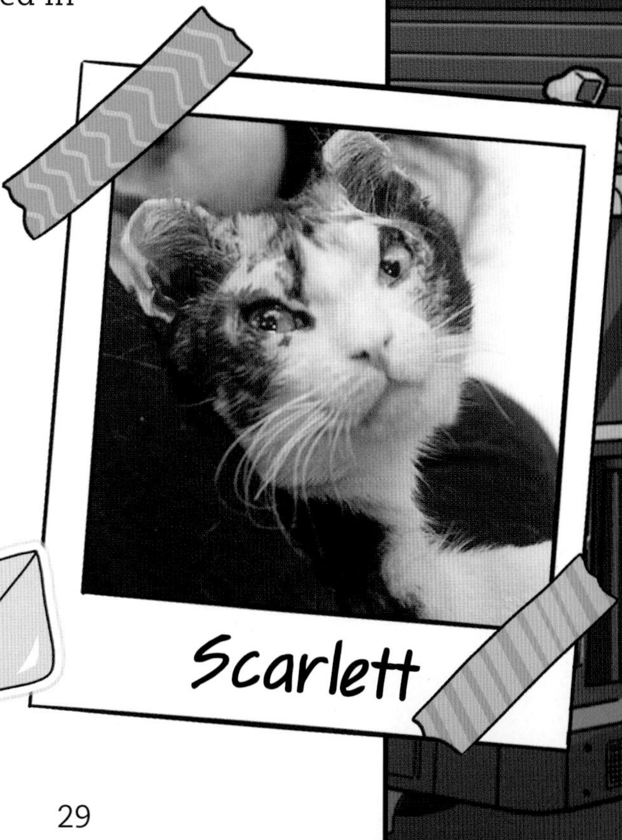
Scarlett

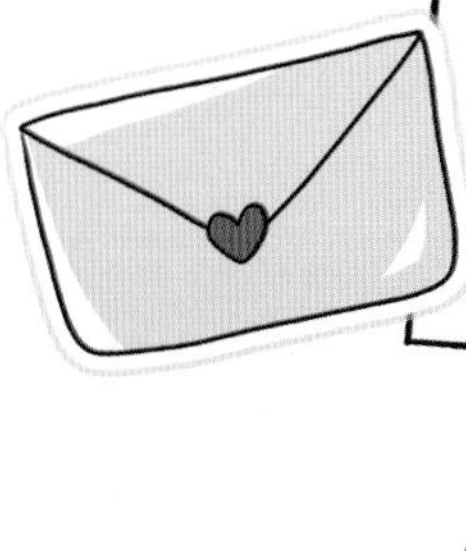

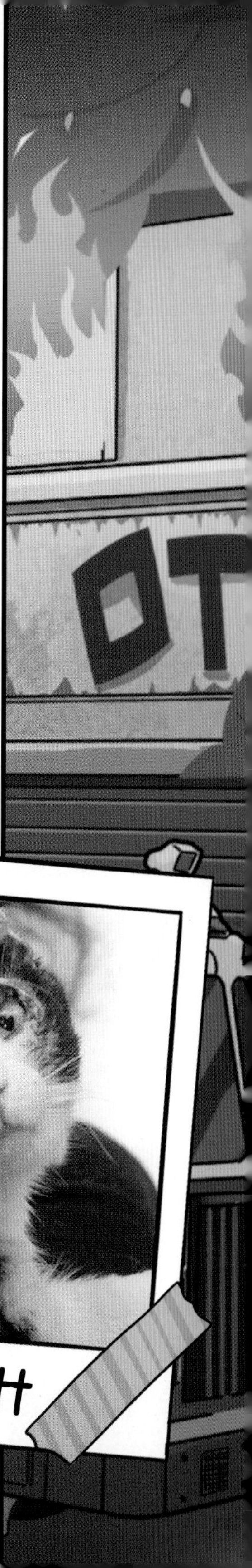

# Glossary

**abandoned**
(uh-BAN-duhnd)
empty or deserted

**adopt** (uh-DOPT)
to take or accept as
one's own, such as a pet

**charcoal** (CHAHR-kohl)
a black form of carbon
left after certain
materials are burned

**engulf** (en-GUHLF)
completely surrounded
or covered by
something

**exhaustion**
(ig-ZAWS-chuhn)
extreme weakness
or tiredness

**musty** (MUHS-tee)
having a stale, moldy,
or damp smell

**recovery**
(ri-KUHV-uh-ree)
to be restored or
returned to health

**territorial**
(ter-ih-TAWR-ee-uhl)
fierce and defensive
of an area claimed as
one's own

**unanimous**
(yoo-NAN-uh-muhs)
agreed on by everyone

# Read More

Berglund, Bruce. *Togo Takes the Lead: Heroic Sled Dog of the Alaska Serum Run*. North Mankato, MN: Capstone Press, 2023.

Loewen, Nancy. *Scarlett the Cat to the Rescue: Fire Hero*. North Mankato, MN: Picture Window Books, 2015.

Manning, Matthew K. *Moko to the Rescue*. North Mankato, MN: Capstone Press, 2023.

# Internet Sites

*Newsweek: Amazing Rescues by Animals*
newsweek.com/amazing-animals-343719

*Scarlett, Blaze Heroine*
purr-n-fur.org.uk/famous/scarlett.html

*Top 10 Heroic Animals: Scarlett the Cat*
content.time.com/time/specials/packages/
article/0,28804,2059858_2059863_2060460,00.html

# About the Author

Photo courtesy of
Dorothy Manning Photography

**Matthew K. Manning** is the author of more than 100 books and dozens of comic books. Some of his favorite projects include the popular comic book crossover *Batman/Teenage Mutant Ninja Turtles Adventures* and the 12-issue series *Marvel Action: Avengers* for IDW, *Exploring Gotham City* for Insight Editions, and the six-volume chapter book series Xander and the Rainbow-Barfing Unicorns for Capstone. Manning lives in Asheville, North Carolina, with his wife, Dorothy, and their two daughters, Lillian and Gwendolyn. Visit him online at www.matthewkmanning.com.

# About the Illustrator

**Alessandro D'urso** was born in 1991 in Formia, Italy, where he currently lives. He studied Comics at Scuola Italiana di Comix. After graduation, he continued his journey as an artist finding inspiration in films from companies such as Disney and Studio Ghibli. He then started his career in illustration, working with different editors to create books for children and teens. In his spare time, Alessandro enjoys reading, watching movies and TV-series, and playing video games.